The SuperCalc3 Companion

COMPUTER COMPANION SERIES

The SuperCalc3 Companion

PETER GOSLING

Paradigm

Paradigm Publishing Ltd.
140 Kensington Church Street
London W8 4BN

First edition 1986

British Library Cataloguing in Publication Data

Gosling, P. E.
The SuperCalc 3 companion.—(Computer companion series)
1. SuperCalc3 (Computer program)
I. Title II. Series
005.36′9 HF5548.4.S86

ISBN 0-948825-01-4

Typeset by Mathematical Composition Setters Ltd, Salisbury and Printed in Great Britain by Hollen Street Press Ltd, Slough, Berks.

About the Series

This series of books fills the need for a source of easy-to-understand guides to the many software packages and computer systems available. Titles will cover microcomputers, operating systems, computer applications, specialised software packages and communications.

Written in a simple and readable style, the books aim to provide a practical working knowledge of the most widely used computing packages to help serious computer users — both in business and at home — make better use of their machines. While these books do not attempt to tell the reader everything about a specific package, they provide an easy familiarisation guide which bridges the gap between the manual and a costly training course.

The authors are experts in their field and proven writers, which ensures accuracy of material and a uniformly high quality of content.

The series presents the information using non-technical language with clear, concise text and contains a variety of carefully structured examples for hands-on experience. The books will be equally useful for the experienced user looking for new applications and for those people looking for new software packages or equipment.

About this Companion

SuperCalc3 (R) is the latest version of the long-running SuperCalc (R) spreadsheet program which has now been extended and improved to provide graph-plotting and data handling. This Companion is divided into three main sections. The first of these deals with the easy parts of spreadsheet handling: the creation of a spreadsheet, entry of data, simple formatting, printing and saving your work. The second section covers more complicated uses of spreadsheets for consolidation of several sheets, replication, user-defined formatting, protection of cells, windowing and titling. The final section covers the plotting of graphs from spreadsheet information, using .XQT files, using your spreadsheet as a database and the transferring of data to and from external programs, for example, transferring data files created using the dBASE II* (R) or dBASE III* (R) programs so that the information they contain can be displayed graphically.

It is assumed that the reader has some experience of using a spreadsheet, not necessarily SuperCalc3, and has at least a nodding acquaintance with the kind of facilities offered by these programs. It is also assumed that the reader is familiar with using a microcomputer belonging to either the IBM PC or the Apricot families.

All those illustrations whose numbers bear an alphabetical suffix are exact copies of what you will see on the screen. All the other illustrations are printer outputs.

Since the preparation of this Companion commenced, Computer Associates have produced Release 2.1 which is an enhanced version of SuperCalc3 and provides a much larger spreadsheet and even more facilities for the user. This version is aimed initially at users of IBM PC and compatible microcomputers.

Contents

Acknowledgements

The author wishes to thank Brian Turner of CETAS Ltd and John Wright of Anglia Telecommunications Ltd for help in the production of this Companion. In addition, grateful thanks are due to Computer Associates for the supply of SuperCalc3, Release 2.1.

The SuperCalc3 Companion

1 Getting started

Entering text and numbers; entering a formula; simple replication; simple formatting; printing and saving your worksheet; a taste of things to come

Entering text and numbers

This chapter is really a swift resume of the general features of SuperCalc3 and is an overview of the things you should be able to do in order to gain the most from this Companion.

When you first start up the SuperCalc3 program you are presented with an empty spreadsheet as shown in Fig. 1.1a. The Width is the width of each column, which is set automatically at startup time to be nine characters. This can be altered at any time for one or more columns. The Memory is the amount of free memory to the nearest K (1024 characters) for your spreadsheet. The Last Col/Row gives the reference of the bottom right-hand cell of the current spreadsheet. Press the ? key and SuperCalc3 will present you with a screenful of helpful information related to your present situation. In Fig. 1.1b you can see the state of the spreadsheet after you have entered various pieces of text. Text can be entered by typing the characters you require to be displayed. There is no need for you to prefix the text with a " symbol. The only time this is necessary is when the text could be confused with a formula. If you needed to enter a date as 12/1/86 you would have it displayed as a decimal

```
  :   A   ::   B   ::   C   ::   D   ::   E   ::   F   ::   G   ::   H   :
 1:
 2:
 3:
 4:
 5:
 6:
 7:
 8:
 9:
10:
11:
12:
13:
14:
15:
16:
17:
18:
19:
20:
> A1
Width:   9   Memory:42 Last Col/Row:A1          ? for Help
  >1
```

Figure 1.1a

number because SuperCalc3 will interpret the slashes as division signs!

The dotted line which occupies Row 5 is obtained by typing the 'repeat text' character, the ', followed by –, which is the character to be repeated across the spreadsheet. In each example, the second line from the bottom of the

```
  :   A   ::   B   ::   C   ::   D   ::   E   ::   F   ::   G   ::   H   :
 1:CASH POSITION
 2:        Jan      Feb      Mar      Apr      May      Jun
 3:Income
 4:Expenditure
 5:-------------------------------------------------------------------------
 6:Amount left
 7:
 8:
 9:
10:
11:
12:
13:
14:
15:
16:
17:
18:
19:
20:
> A1        Text="CASH POSITION
Width:   9  Memory:41 Last Col/Row:G6        ? for Help
  1>
```

Figure 1.1b

```
  !  A   !!   B   !!   C   !!   D   !!   E   !!   F   !!   G   !!   H   !
 1!CASH POSITION
 2!         Jan      Feb      Mar      Apr      May      Jun
 3!Income         1500     1750     1900     1245     1650     1700
 4!Expenditu       850      900     2000     1500      890      950
 5!-----------------------------------------------------------------
 6!Amount left
 7!
 8!
 9!
10!
11!
12!
13!
14!
15!
16!
17!
18!
19!
20!
> A1        Text="CASH POSITION
Width:  9   Memory: 41 Last Col/Row:G6     ? for Help
  1>
```

Figure 1.1c

screen tells you the current cell being highlighted and what its contents are.

Now we enter numbers into the block of cells known to SuperCalc3 as B3:G4 (specified by the upper left and lower right cell references) and the result is shown in Fig. 1.1c. You may notice that the text in A4 is truncated. This is because

```
  !  A   !!   B   !!   C   !!   D   !!   E   !!   F   !!   G   !!   H   !
 1!CASH POSITION
 2!         Jan      Feb      Mar      Apr      May      Jun
 3!Income         1500     1750     1900     1245     1650     1700
 4!Expenditu       850      900     2000     1500      890      950
 5!-----------------------------------------------------------------
 6!Amount le       650
 7!
 8!
 9!
10!
11!
12!
13!
14!
15!
16!
17!
18!
19!
20!
< B6        Form=B3-B4
To? (Enter Range), the <RETURN>; or <,> for Options
 20>/Replicate,B6,c6:g6
```

Figure 1.1d

```
   :  A  ::  B  ::  C  ::  D  ::  E  ::  F  ::  G  ::  H  :
  1:CASH POSITION
  2:        Jan      Feb      Mar      Apr      May      Jun
  3:Income        1500     1750     1900     1245     1650     1700
  4:Expenditu      850      900     2000     1500      890      950
  5:------------------------------------------------------------------
  6:Amount le      650      850     -100     -255      760      750
  7:
  8:
  9:
 10:
 11:
 12:
 13:
 14:
 15:
 16:
 17:
 18:
 19:
 20:
< A1        Text="CASH POSITION
Width:  9  Memory: 41  Last Col/Row:G6      ? for Help
  1>
```

Figure 1.1e

the cell immediately to its right is now occupied so that the text from the tenth character onward is not displayed. It is not lost, but is simply too long to fit into the space allotted to it. We will deal with this shortly.

```
   :  A  ::  B  ::  C  ::  D  ::  E  ::  F  ::  G  ::  H  :
  1:CASH POSITION
  2:        Jan      Feb      Mar      Apr      May      Jun
  3:Income        1500     1750     1900     1245     1650     1700
  4:Expenditu      850      900     2000     1500      890      950
  5:------------------------------------------------------------------
  6:Amount le      650      850     -100     -255      760      750
  7:
  8:
  9:
 10:
 11:
 12:
 13:
 14:
 15:
 16:
 17:
 18:
 19:
 20:
< A1        Text="CASH POSITION
Define Formats: (I,G,E,£,R,L,TR,TL,*,U(1-8),H,D,column width)
 18>/Format,Column,A,
```

Figure 1.1f

```
  :     A     ::    B    ::    C    ::    D    ::    E    ::    F    ::    G    ::    H    :
 1:CASH POSITION
 2:              Jan       Feb       Mar       Apr       May       Jun
 3:Income          1500      1750      1900      1245      1650      1700
 4:Expenditure      850       900      2000      1500       890       950
 5:-------------------------------------------------------------------------------
 6:Amount left      650       850      -100      -255       760       750
 7:
 8:
 9:
10:
11:
12:
13:
14:
15:
16:
17:
18:
19:
20:
< A1
Width:12  Memory: 41 Last Col/Row:G6      ? for Help
 1>
```

Figure 1.1g

Entering a formula

Next we need to calculate the amount left each month by taking the Expenditure away from the Income in each column. You should notice that the formula has been entered into cell B6, as you can see in Fig. 1.1d, and consists of a

```
  :     A     ::    B    ::    C    ::    D    ::    E    ::    F    ::    G    ::    H    :
 1:CASH POSITION
 2:              Jan       Feb       Mar       Apr       May       Jun
 3:Income          1500      1750      1900      1245      1650      1700
 4:Expenditure      850       900      2000      1500       890       950
 5:-------------------------------------------------------------------------------
 6:Amount left      650       850      -100      -255       760       750
 7:
 8:
 9:
10:
11:
12:
13:
14:
15:
16:
17:
18:
19:
20:
< A6          Text="Amount left
Define Formats: (I,G,E,£,R,L,TR,TL,*,U(1-8),H,D,column width)
 32>/Format,Column,b:g,TextRight,£
```

Figure 1.1h

```
  |     A      ||    B    ||    C    ||    D    ||    E    ||    F    ||    G    ||    H    |
 1|CASH POSITION
 2|                   Jan       Feb       Mar       Apr       May       Jun
 3|Income         1500.00   1750.00   1900.00   1245.00   1650.00   1700.00
 4|Expenditure     850.00    900.00   2000.00   1500.00    890.00    950.00
 5|------------------------------------------------------------------------------------
 6|Amount left     650.00    850.00   -100.00   -255.00    760.00    750.00
 7|
 8|
 9|
10|
11|
12|
13|
14|
15|
16|
17|
18|
19|
20|
< A6          Text="Amount left
Width: 12  Memory: 41   Last Col/Row:G6    ? for Help
  1>
```

Figure 1.1i

statement which consists of cell references only. What it is saying is, of course, that the contents of cell B4 should be taken from the contents of cell B3. You should note that it is the result of this subtraction which is displayed (650 in this case) in cell B6, yet the cell actually contains a Formula (Form in SuperCalc3 language). What we need to do now is to copy this formula along the row from C6 to G6 and this

```
  |     A      ||    B    ||    C    ||    D    ||    E    ||    F    ||    G    ||    H    |
 1|CASH POSITION
 2|                   Jan       Feb       Mar       Apr       May       Jun
 3|Income         1500.00   1750.00   1900.00   1245.00   1650.00   1700.00
 4|Expenditure     850.00    900.00   2000.00   1500.00    890.00    950.00
 5|------------------------------------------------------------------------------------
 6|Amount left     650.00    850.00   -100.00   -255.00    760.00    750.00
 7|
 8|Total profit over 6 months:
 9|
10|
11|
12|
13|
14|
15|
16|
17|
18|
19|
20|
> D8
Width: 9   Memory: 41  Last Col/Row:G8    ? for Help
 11>sum(b6:g6)
```

Figure 1.1j

```
   !     A     !!    B    !!    C    !!    D    !!    E    !!    F    !!    G    !!    H    !
  1!CASH POSITION
  2!                   Jan      Feb        Mar        Apr        May        Jun
  3!Income         1500.00  1750.00    1900.00    1245.00    1650.00    1700.00
  4!Expenditure     850.00   900.00    2000.00    1500.00     890.00     950.00
  5!----------------------------------------------------------------------------
  6!Amount left     650.00   850.00    -100.00    -255.00     760.00     750.00
  7!
  8!Total profit over 6 months:        2655.00
  9!
 10!
 11!
 12!
 13!
 14!
 15!
 16!
 17!
 18!
 19!
 20!
> E8
Width:  9  Memory: 41 Last Col/Row:G8    ? for Help
  >1
```

Figure 1.1k

is dealt with next. If you look at Fig. 1.1j you will see that the spreadsheet has an extra entry showing the total profit over six months with the formula

SUM(B6:G6)

entered into D8. The result is shown in Fig. 1.1k. The next two sections show how we actually get there with our sheet laid out exactly as we want it.

```
CASH POSITION
                   Jan      Feb        Mar        Apr        May        Jun
Income         1500.00  1750.00    1900.00    1245.00    1650.00    1700.00
Expenditure     850.00   900.00    2000.00    1500.00     890.00     950.00
----------------------------------------------------------------------------
Amount left     650.00   850.00    -100.00    -255.00     760.00     750.00

Total profit over 6 months:        2655.00




> A1
Enter Range
 20>/Output,Display,all
```

Figure 1.1l

```
  :    A    ::   B   ::   C   ::   D   ::   E   ::   F   ::   G   ::  H  :
 1:CASH POSITION
 2:                 Jan       Feb       Mar       Apr       May       Jun
 3:Income       1500.00   1750.00   1900.00   1010.00   1650.00   1700.00
 4:Expenditure   850.00    900.00   2000.00   1500.00    890.00    950.00
 5:---------------------------------------------------------------------------
 6:Amount left   650.00    850.00   -100.00   -490.00    760.00    750.00
 7:
 8:Total profit over 6 months:      2420.00
 9:
10:
11:
12:
13:
14:
15:
16:
17:
18:
19:
20:
^ E2        Text="Apr
Width:  9  Memory: 41 Last Col/Row:G8    ? for Help
 >1
```

Figure 1.1m

Simple replication

By pressing the / key you are presented with the list of Command options on the first line from the bottom. Each letter represents a different command and the one wanted in this case is R (Replicate), the object being to copy the formula in B6 into the five cells to its right. On pressing /R SuperCalc3 responds with the prompt shown in Fig. 1.1d together with the reply. It says that you want to copy the formula held in cell B6 into the range C6:G6. Notice that SuperCalc3 does not mind whether these are entered in upper or lower case characters. Press the Return key and the result seen almost immediately is shown in Fig. 1.1e. If you examine the contents of the cells into which the formula has been replicated you will see that they contain the formulae C3-C4, D3-D4 and so on. SuperCalc3 has adjusted the references for you. There will be further reference to the powerful replication command, together with Copy, in later chapters.

Simple formatting

You now want to be able to make everything you have entered onto the spreadsheet visible and laid out neatly. The first requirement is to widen Column A using the Format command, /F, followed by the selection of the C(olumn) option. SuperCalc3 asks which column you want and by pressing the Return key you find that the current column label is entered automatically. If you needed to change a range of columns you could enter their labels as, for example, A:G. Then the screen becomes as shown in Fig. 1.1f. This allows you to specify the format, or layout, of the specified column. You want to widen the column to twelve characters, so 12 is entered and after the Return key has been pressed the screen appears as shown in Fig. 1.1g. Now you want to do two things. The first is to change the position of the text relative to the numbers in the columns and, secondly, because you are dealing with money, you want to display the numbers in money format. As you are almost always going to be dealing with decimal amounts of money, then you are going to need a display with a decimal point after the units digit and two decimal places after that. Select columns B:G (that is B through G), TR for Text Right and the £ option. SuperCalc3 does not mind, by the way, if the column identification letters are entered in upper or lower case. The options available are shown in Fig. 1.1h. Notice how they string along behind one another. Press Return and the display becomes as shown in Fig. 1.1i.

Printing and saving your worksheet

Having created your worksheet to your satisfaction, you will want to print it out. First of all you will want to get rid of the border showing the column letters and row numbers. You do this by the /GB (Global command, Border option) to switch the border off. Then you can print the sheet on your printer by choosing the /O (Output) command and specifying the extent of the sheet and choosing the Display option in order to get the result as shown in Fig. 1.1l.

To save the sheet choose the /S (Save) command and name it when requested. SuperCalc3 will automatically save your worksheet under that name and with a .CAL extension.

A taste of things to come

In Fig. 1.1m you can see what happens to the spreadsheet when just one entry is changed. In this case it is the contents of E3 where the figure of 1245 has become 1010. Without any prompt from you, apart from changing the number, the entire spreadsheet is recalculated. You can see how useful that feature is because it allows you, with the minimum of effort, to indulge in the game of 'what happens if . . .'. Usually a game which is far too costly in time and effort to do under the tyranny of the old-fashioned pencil, paper, rubber and, indeed, pocket calculator.

Additional ways of displaying the information stored in a SuperCalc3 spreadsheet are shown in Figs. 1.2, 1.3 and 1.4. The first two of these graphs display one's change of fortune over the first six months of the year. The bar chart in Fig. 1.2 demonstrates clearly the times when expenditure has

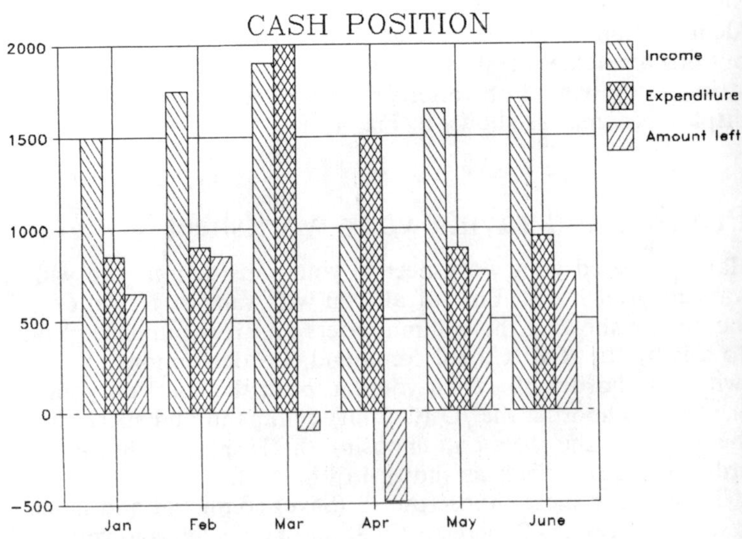

Figure 1.2

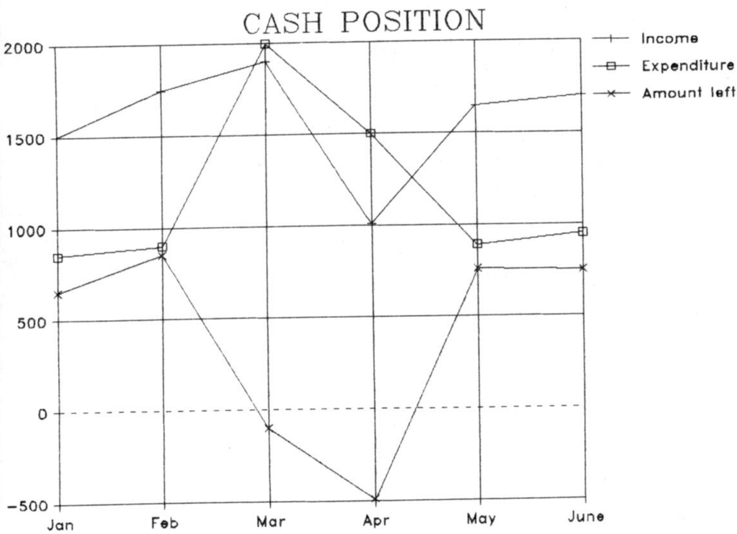

Figure 1.3

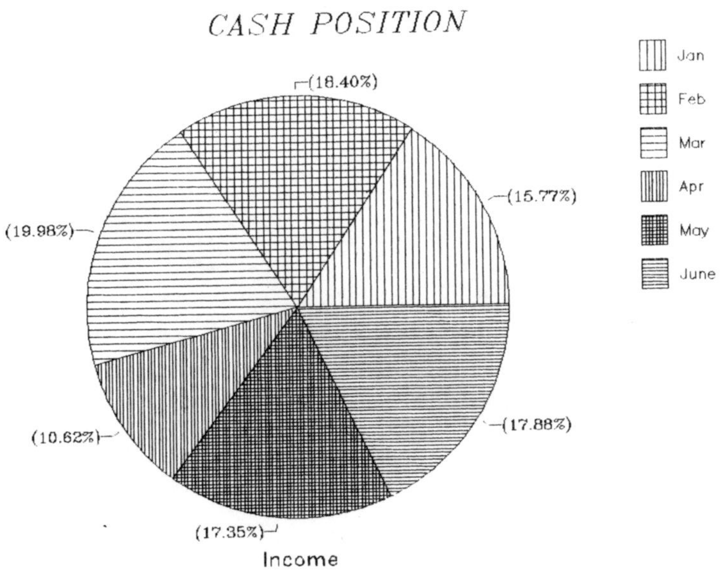

Figure 1.4

exceeded income. The line graph in Fig. 1.3 shows the same information in a similar manner; the dip below the zero line shows the bad months. The third graph is a pie chart showing the relative states of income over the six months with the percentages of the total income over the period printed beside each 'slice' of the pie. With very little effort, once you have mastered the techniques, you can display your information in a wide range of graphical forms. These are covered in Chapter 7.

2 Using Replicate and Copy

Example 1 — part 1; Example 2 — part 1

The examples commenced in this chapter will be developed over a number of chapters as more and more SuperCalc3 facilities are used. You should note that the column and row numbers have been left in for the majority of the illustrations in order for you to identify entries more easily.

Example 1 — Setting up a cash flow spreadsheet — part 1

A company called A.B.C. Computers Ltd are going to produce a cash flow analysis for the years 1986 through 1991 and the spreadsheet devised to do this starts off as is shown in Fig. 2.1 with the basic information entered. The first figure is the starting revenue and the projected percentage growths for the succeeding years are entered as decimal numbers. You should note that column A is too narrow to contain all the text required. At present you can see all the contents of the column. But when entries are made in column C you will lose some of the display. So column A has been widened so that the sheet looks as shown in Fig. 2.2.

The screen display shown in Fig. 2.2a shows the formula entered in E6 which will calculate the 1986 figure for revenue based on a 15 per cent growth. This is to be replicated across

```
  :   A   ::   B   ::   C   ::   D   ::   E   ::   F   ::   G   ::   H   ::   I   ::   J   :
 1:PROJECTED CASH FLOW - (Thousands)    A.B.C.Computers Ltd
 2:
 3:
 4:YEARS:                              1985     1986     1987     1988     1989     1990     1991
 5:                            ------------------------------------------------------------------
 6:Revenue                            12500
 7:% growth                                      .15      .20      .30      .15      .10      .10
 8:
 9:PRODUCTION COSTS
10:Wages
11:Materials
12:N.I. and Pensions
13:Packaging & Miscel
14:
15:SALES & OFFICE EXPENSES
16:Marketing staff salaries
17:Office staff salaries
18:N.I. & Pensions
19:Advertising
20:Depreciation
21:Miscellaneous
22:                            ------------------------------------------------------------------
23:Total operating expenses
24:Interest
25:Pre-Tax income
26:Tax
27:Net income
```

Figure 2.1

```
  |              A            ||  B  ||  C  ||  D  ||  E  ||  F  ||  G  ||  H  ||  I  ||  J  |
 1|PROJECTED CASH FLOW - (Thousands)             A.B.C.Computers Ltd
 2|
 3|
 4|YEARS:                                            1985   1986   1987   1988   1989   1990   1991
 5|                                             ------------------------------------------------------
 6|Revenue                                          12500
 7|% growth                                                  .15    .20    .30    .15    .10    .10
 8|
 9|PRODUCTION COSTS
10|Wages
11|Materials
12|N.I. and Pensions
13|Packaging & Miscellaneous
14|
15|SALES & OFFICE EXPENSES
16|Marketing staff salaries
17|Office staff salaries
18|N.I. & Pensions
19|Advertising
20|Depreciation
21|Miscellaneous
22|                                                ------------------------------------------------------
23|Total operating expenses
24|Interest repayable
25|Pre-Tax income
26|Tax
27|Net income
```

Figure 2.2

```
  ¦   B   ¦¦          C          ¦¦    D    ¦¦    E    ¦¦    F    ¦¦    G    ¦¦    H    ¦
 1¦ds)                                        A.B.C.Computers Ltd
 2¦
 3¦
 4¦                                    1985      1986      1987      1988      1989
 5¦                              ------------------------------------------------------
 6¦                                   12500
 7¦                                              .15       .20       .30       .15
 8¦
 9¦
10¦         of Revenue
11¦         of Revenue
12¦         of Wages
13¦         Growth rate
14¦
15¦
16¦         of Revenue
17¦         Growth rate
18¦         of total salaries
19¦         of Revenue
20¦Fixed Annual amount
< E6        Form=D6*(1+E7)
To? (Enter Range), then <RETURN>; or <,> for Options
 20>/Replicate,E6,F6:J6
```

Figure 2.2a

the rest of the columns. Replicate is used here, not Copy, since only the former can be used to copy into a range of cells. No Options are requested since you should take advantage of the automatic adjustment that Replicate offers. The result of this replication is shown in Fig. 2.3 where by using /GF (the Global command followed by the Formula option) you display the contents of the cells rather than what is displayed.

Also in Fig. 2.3 you will see that the textual information which displays the way in which the various expenses have been arrived at has been added. (This is in column C which has had to be widened in order to show all the information.) For example, the wages of the workers engaged in production is 19% of the total revenue, the National Insurance and Pensions costs are 20% of the wages bill and so on. The percentages are in column B and these are used to produce the changes in wages and other costs. The first three formulae needed to produce the 1986 figures for Wages, Materials and National Insurance and Pensions have also been entered.

The display shown in Fig. 2.3a gives the state of the screen just prior to the replication of the three new formulae, and Fig. 2.4 shows the final result. Note that the command string

```
   |            A             ||  B  ||         C          ||   D   ||   E   ||   F   ||   G   ||   H   ||   I   ||   J   |
 1|PROJECTED CASH FLOW - (Thousands)                                  A.B.C.Computers Ltd
 2|
 3|
 4|YEARS:                                                     1985     1986     1987     1988     1989     1990     1991
 5|
   ---------------------------------------------------------------------------------------------------------------------
 6|Revenue                                                    12500    D6*(1+E7 E6*(1+F7 F6*(1+G7 G6*(1+H7 H6*(1+I7 I6*(1+J7
 7|% growth                                                             .15      .2       .3       .15      .1       .1
 8|
 9|PRODUCTION COSTS
10|Wages                          .19      of Revenue                   E6*B10
11|Materials                      .15      of Revenue                   E6*B11
12|N.I. and Pensions              .2       of Wages                     B12*E10
13|Packaging & Miscellaneous      .07      Growth rate
14|
15|SALES & OFFICE EXPENSES
16|Marketing staff salaries       .08      of Revenue
17|Office staff salaries          .1       Growth rate
18|N.I. & Pensions                .2       of total salaries
19|Advertising                    .35      of Revenue
20|Depreciation                            Fixed Annual amount
21|Miscellaneous                  19       Annual fixed increase
22|                                                           -----------------------------------------------------------
23|Total operating expenses
24|Interest repayable            Fixed Annual amount
25|Pre-Tax income
26|Tax                                     of Pre-Tax Income
27|Net income
```

Figure 2.3

```
    :  B  ::         C          ::  D  ::  E  ::  F  ::  G  ::  H  :
  3:
  4:                                1985     1986     1987     1988     1989
  5:                             ----------------------------------------------
  6:                                12500    14375    17250    22425    25789
  7:                                           .15      .20      .30      .15
  8:
  9:
 10: .19      of Revenue                    2731.25
 11: .15      of Revenue                    2156.25
 12: .2       of Wages                       546.25
 13: .07      Growth rate
 14:
 15:
 16: .08      of Revenue
 17: .1       Growth rate
 18: .2       of total salaries
 19: .35      of Revenue
 20:Fixed Annual amount
 21: 19       Annual fixed increase
 22:                             ----------------------------------------------
^ E10          Form=E6*B10
N(o Adjust), A(sk for Adjust), V(alues), +, -, *, /
 28>Replicate,E10:E12,F10,J10,
```

Figure 2.3a

at the bottom of the screen needs a comma at the end since you do not want every entry in the formula being replicated to be adjusted for you. All references to entries in column B must remain the same in every replication.

Figure 2.5 shows a section of the sheet giving the other formulae needed to start off the expenses section of the cash flow. Notice that the contents of E17 have a starting figure as does the Miscellaneous entry where there is an expected fixed annual increase. In Fig. 2.5a the contents of E16 are copied, not replicated, into F16. The comma at the end of the command shows that you need to stop at least one entry in the formula from being automatically adjusted. In this case it is the B16 entry. The contents of all the other empty cells in column F are similarly copied. This makes up a solid block of cells ready to be replicated across the rest of the sheet as shown in Fig. 2.5b. You should notice the comma at the end of the bottom line of the screen which indicates that adjustments will have to be made to some formula entries while others are to remain constant. For example, the B16 in the formula in cell F16 must remain the same right across the sheet, but the F6 must become G6 and H6 in turn.

The remainder of the sheet is completed by summing the expenses and subtracting from the revenues for each year, with the result as shown in Fig. 2.6.

	A	B	C	D	E	F	G	H	I	J
1	PROJECTED CASH FLOW - (Thousands)				A.B.C.Computers Ltd					
2										
3										
4	YEARS:			1985	1986	1987	1988	1989	1990	1991
5										
6	Revenue			12500	14375	17250	22425	25789	28368	31204
7	% growth				.15	.20	.30	.15	.10	.10
8										
9	PRODUCTION COSTS									
10	Wages	.19	of Revenue		2731.25	3277.5	4260.75	4899.863	5389.849	5928.834
11	Materials	.15	of Revenue		2156.25	2587.5	3363.75	3868.313	4255.144	4680.658
12	N.I. and Pensions	.2	of Wages		546.25	655.5	852.15	979.9725	1077.970	1185.767
13	Packaging & Miscellaneous	.07	Growth rate		115	123.05	131.6635	140.8799	150.7415	161.2934
14										
15	SALES & OFFICE EXPENSES									
16	Marketing staff salaries	.08	of Revenue							
17	Office staff salaries	.1	Growth rate							
18	N.I. & Pensions	.2	of total salaries							
19	Advertising	.35	of Revenue							
20	Depreciation		Fixed Annual amount							
21	Miscellaneous	£19	Annual fixed increase							
22										
23	Total operating expenses									
24	Interest repayable	Fixed Annual amount								
25	Pre-Tax income									
26	Tax		of Pre-Tax Income							
27	Net income									

Figure 2.4

	A	B	C	D	E	F	G	H	I	J
14										
15	SALES & OFFICE EXPENSES									
16	Marketing staff salaries	.08	of Revenue		E6*B16					
17	Office staff salaries	.1	Growth rate		1200	E17*(1+B17)				
18	N.I. & Pensions	.2	of total salaries		(E17+E16)*B18					
19	Advertising	.35	of Revenue		E6*B19					
20	Depreciation		Fixed Annual amount		20					
21	Miscellaneous	£19	Annual fixed increase		19	E21+B21				
22										

Figure 2.5

```
   |  B  ||          C          || D  ||  E  ||  F  ||  G  ||  H  |
  3|
  4|                                1985      1986      1987      1988      1989
  5|                            --------------------------------------------------
  6|                                12500     14375     17250     22425     25789
  7|                                            .15       .20       .30       .15
  8|
  9|
 10| .19      of Revenue                    2731.25    3277.5   4260.75  4899.863
 11| .15      of Revenue                    2156.25    2587.5   3363.75  3868.313
 12| .2       of Wages                       546.25     655.5    852.15  979.9725
 13| .07      Growth rate                       115    123.05  131.6635  140.8799
 14|
 15|
 16| .08      of Revenue                   1150
 17| .1       Growth rate                  1200       1320
 18| .2       of total salaries             470
 19| .35      of Revenue                 5031.25
 20|Fixed Annual amount                      20
 21| 19       Annual fixed increase          19         38
 22|                            --------------------------------------------------
< E16          Form=E6*B16
N(o Adjust), A(sk for Adjust), V(alues), +, -, *, /
 15>/Copy,E16,F16,
```

Figure 2.5a

Figure 2.7 shows the final result with the net income calculated on the basis of a 48 per cent rate of tax. The printout shown in Fig. 2.8 shows the contents of every cell in order to provide the display shown in the previous figure. It was done by using the /G (Global) command followed by the F option. This example will be returned to in the next chapter when formatting your displays is covered.

```
   |  B  ||          C          || D  ||  E  ||  F  ||  G  ||  H  |
  3|
  4|                                1985      1986      1987      1988      1989
  5|                            --------------------------------------------------
  6|                                12500     14375     17250     22425     25789
  7|                                            .15       .20       .30       .15
  8|
  9|
 10| .19      of Revenue                    2731.25    3277.5   4260.75  4899.863
 11| .15      of Revenue                    2156.25    2587.5   3363.75  3868.313
 12| .2       of Wages                       546.25     655.5    852.15  979.9725
 13| .07      Growth rate                       115    123.05  131.6635  140.8799
 14|
 15|
 16| .08      of Revenue                   1150       1380
 17| .1       Growth rate                  1200       1320
 18| .2       of total salaries             470        540
 19| .35      of Revenue                 5031.25    6037.5
 20|Fixed Annual amount                      20         20
 21| 19       Annual fixed increase          19         38
 22|                            --------------------------------------------------
v F16          Form=F6*B16
N(o Adjust), A(sk for Adjust), V(alues), +, -, *, /
 28>/Replicate,F16:F21,G16:J16,
```

Figure 2.5b

	A	B	C	D	E	F	G	H	I	J
1	PROJECTED CASH FLOW - (Thousands)				A.B.C.Computers Ltd					
2										
3										
4	YEARS:			1985	1986	1987	1988	1989	1990	1991
5										
6	Revenue			12500	14375	17250	22425	25789	28368	31204
7	% growth				.15	.20	.30	.15	.10	.10
8										
9	PRODUCTION COSTS									
10	Wages	.19	of Revenue		2731.25	3277.5	4260.75	4899.863	5389.849	5928.834
11	Materials	.15	of Revenue		2156.25	2587.5	3363.75	3868.313	4255.144	4680.658
12	N.I. and Pensions	.2	of Wages		546.25	655.5	852.15	979.9725	1077.970	1185.767
13	Packaging & Miscellaneous	.07	Growth rate		115	123.05	131.6635	140.8799	150.7415	161.2934
14										
15	SALES & OFFICE EXPENSES									
16	Marketing staff salaries	.08	of Revenue		1150	1380	1794	2063.1	2269.41	2496.351
17	Office staff salaries	.1	Growth rate		1200	1320	1452	1597.2	1756.92	1932.612
18	N.I. & Pensions	.2	of total salaries		470	540	649.2	732.06	805.266	885.7926
19	Advertising	.35	of Revenue		5031.25	6037.5	7848.75	9026.063	9928.669	10921.54
20	Depreciation		Fixed Annual amount		20	20	20	20	20	20
21	Miscellaneous	£19	Annual fixed increase		19	38	57	76	95	114
22										
23	Total operating expenses			6400	9557.75	11321.55	14374.51	16440.49	18089.71	19901.66
24	Interest repayable	Fixed Annual amount								
25	Pre-Tax income									
26	Tax		of Pre-Tax Income							
27	Net income									

Figure 2.6

	A	B	C	D	E	F	G	H	I	J
1	PROJECTED CASH FLOW - (Thousands)				A.B.C.Computers Ltd					
2										
3										
4	YEARS:									
5				1985	1986	1987	1988	1989	1990	1991
6	Revenue									
7	% growth			12500	14375	17250	22425	25789	28368	31204
8					.15	.20	.30	.15	.10	.10
9	PRODUCTION COSTS									
10	Wages	.19	of Revenue							
11	Materials	.15	of Revenue		2731.25	3277.5	4260.75	4899.863	5389.849	5928.834
12	N.I. and Pensions	.2	of Wages		2156.25	2587.5	3363.75	3868.313	4255.144	4680.658
13	Packaging & Miscellaneous	.07	Growth rate		546.25	655.5	852.15	979.9725	1077.970	1185.767
14					115	123.05	131.6635	140.8799	150.7415	161.2934
15	SALES & OFFICE EXPENSES									
16	Marketing staff salaries	.08	of Revenue							
17	Office staff salaries	.1	Growth rate		1150	1380	1794	2063.1	2269.41	2496.351
18	N.I. & Pensions	.2	of total salaries		1200	1320	1452	1597.2	1756.92	1932.612
19	Advertising	.35	of Revenue		470	540	649.2	732.06	805.266	885.7926
20	Depreciation		Fixed Annual amount		5031.25	6037.5	7848.75	9026.063	9928.669	10921.54
21	Miscellaneous	£19	Annual fixed increase		20	20	20	20	20	20
22					19	38	57	76	95	114
23	Total operating expenses									
24	Interest repayable	Fixed Annual amount		6400	9557.75	11321.55	14374.51	16440.49	18089.71	19901.66
25	Pre-Tax income			13	13	13	13	13	13	13
26	Tax	.48	of Pre-Tax Income	6087	4804.25	5915.45	8037.487	9335.263	10264.92	11289.73
27	Net income			2921.76	2306.04	2839.416	3857.994	4480.926	4927.159	5419.070
				3165.24	2498.21	3076.034	4179.493	4854.337	5337.756	5870.659

Figure 2.7

	A	B	C	D	E	F	G	H	I	J
1	PROJECTED CASH FLOW - (Thousands)				A.B.C.Computers Ltd					
2										
3										
4	YEARS:			1985	1986	1987	1988	1989	1990	1991
5										
6	Revenue			12500	D6*(1+E7)	E6*(1+F7)	F6*(1+G7)	G6*(1+H7)	H6*(1+I7)	I6*(1+J7)
7	% growth				.15	.2	.3	.15	.1	.1
8										
9	PRODUCTION COSTS									
10	Wages	.19	of Revenue		E6*B10	F6*B10	G6*B10	H6*B10	I6*B10	J6*B10
11	Materials	.15	of Revenue		E6*B11	F6*B11	G6*B11	H6*B11	I6*B11	J6*B11
12	N.I. and Pensions	.2	of Wages		B12*E10	B12*F10	B12*G10	B12*H10	B12*I10	B12*J10
13	Packaging & Miscellaneous	.07	Growth rate		115	E13*(1+B13)	F13*(1+B13)	G13*(1+B13)	H13*(1+B13)	I13*(1+B13)
14										
15	SALES & OFFICE EXPENSES									
16	Marketing staff salaries	.08	of Revenue		E6*B16	F6*B16	G6*B16	H6*B16	I6*B16	J6*B16
17	Office staff salaries	.1	Growth rate		1200	E17*(1+B17)	F17*(1+B17)	G17*(1+B17)	H17*(1+B17)	I17*(1+B17)
18	N.I. & Pensions	.2	of total salaries		(E17+E16)*B18	(F17+F16)*B18	(G17+G16)*B18	(H17+H16)*B18	(I17+I16)*B18	(J17+J16)*B18
19	Advertising	.35	of Revenue		E6*B19	F6*B19	G6*B19	H6*B19	I6*B19	J6*B19
20	Depreciation		Fixed Annual amount		20	20	20	20	20	20
21	Miscellaneous	£19	Annual fixed increase		19	E21+B21	F21+B21	G21+B21	H21+B21	I21+B21
22										
23	Total operating expenses			6400	SUM(E11:E13,E17:E21)	SUM(F11:F13,F17:F21)	SUM(G11:G13,G17:G21)	SUM(H11:H13,H17:H21)	SUM(I11:I13,I17:I21)	SUM(J11:J13,J17:J21)
24	Interest repayable	Fixed Annual amount		13	13	13	13	13	13	13
25	Pre-Tax income			D6-D23-D24	E6-E23-E24	F6-F23-F24	G6-G23-G24	H6-H23-H24	I6-I23-I24	J6-J23-J24
26	Tax	.48	of Pre-Tax Income	D25*B26	E25*B26	F25*B26	G25*B26	H25*B26	I25*B26	J25*B26
27	Net income			D25-D26	E25-E26	F25-F26	G25-G26	H25-H26	I25-I26	J25-J26

Figure 2.8

Example 2 — A time series — part 1

In this example, which will be developed over several chapters, you are going to make a statistical prediction of the next year's production of a company based on past production figures. The information is first of all displayed in the usual spreadsheet table, but later on in Chapter 7 it will be displayed in graphical form. The first part of the spreadsheet lists the quarterly production for the years 1978 to 1981 and the output, **p**, for those quarters. The time, **t**, is measured from an assumed mean which is the fourth quarter of 1979. The formula to calculate this time difference is then replicated down column D as is shown in Fig. 2.9a.

Figure 2.9b shows the next two columns, **p** × **t** and **t** squared, set up and replicated down columns E and F. Notice that SuperCalc3 does the adjustment for you and so you do not ask for the options. The final result of these calculations is shown in the screen display in Fig. 2.9c. All that remains to be done for this part of the operation is to sum each of the columns, and the final result is shown in Fig. 2.9d.

The basic data is now on the sheet and the rest of the

```
   !   A   !!      B      !!      C      !!      D      !!   E   !!   F   !!   G   !
  1!                       Output - p     Time - t
  2!1978 1st Quarter        19             -7
  3!1978 2nd Quarter        13             -6
  4!1978 3rd Quarter        9
  5!1978 4th Quarter        18
  6!1979 1st Quarter        22
  7!1979 2nd Quarter        15
  8!1979 3rd Quarter        14
  9!1979 4th Quarter        23
 10!1980 1st Quarter        27
 11!1980 2nd Quarter        17
 12!1980 3rd Quarter        16
 13!1980 4th Quarter        27
 14!1981 1st Quarter        31
 15!1981 2nd Quarter        20
 16!1981 3rd Quarter        19
 17!1981 4th Quarter        27
 18!
 19!
 20!
^ D3         Form=D2+1
To? (Enter Range), then <RETURN>; or <,> for Options
 21>/Replicate,D3,d4:d17
```

Figure 2.9a

```
   !   A   !!    B    !!     C     !!     D     !!   E   !!    F   !!   G   !
  1!                     Output - p    Time - t    p * t       t^2
  2!1978 1st Quarter    19          -7              -133        49
  3!1978 2nd Quarter    13          -6
  4!1978 3rd Quarter    9           -5
  5!1978 4th Quarter    18          -4
  6!1979 1st Quarter    22          -3
  7!1979 2nd Quarter    15          -2
  8!1979 3rd Quarter    14          -1
  9!1979 4th Quarter    23           0
 10!1980 1st Quarter    27           1
 11!1980 2nd Quarter    17           2
 12!1980 3rd Quarter    16           3
 13!1980 4th Quarter    27           4
 14!1981 1st Quarter    31           5
 15!1981 2nd Quarter    20           6
 16!1981 3rd Quarter    19           7
 17!1981 4th Quarter    27           8
 18!
 19!
 20!
^ E2        Form=C2*D2
To? (Enter Range), then <RETURN>; or <,> for Options
 24>/Replicate,E2:F2,E3:E17
```

Figure 2.9b

```
   !   A   !!    B    !!     C     !!     D     !!   E   !!    F   !!   G   !
  1!                     Output - p    Time - t    p * t       t^2
  2!1978 1st Quarter    19          -7              -133        49
  3!1978 2nd Quarter    13          -6               -78        36
  4!1978 3rd Quarter    9           -5               -45        25
  5!1978 4th Quarter    18          -4               -72        16
  6!1979 1st Quarter    22          -3               -66         9
  7!1979 2nd Quarter    15          -2               -30         4
  8!1979 3rd Quarter    14          -1               -14         1
  9!1979 4th Quarter    23           0                 0         0
 10!1980 1st Quarter    27           1                27         1
 11!1980 2nd Quarter    17           2                34         4
 12!1980 3rd Quarter    16           3                48         9
 13!1980 4th Quarter    27           4               108        16
 14!1981 1st Quarter    31           5               155        25
 15!1981 2nd Quarter    20           6               120        36
 16!1981 3rd Quarter    19           7               133        49
 17!1981 4th Quarter    27           8               216        64
 18!
 19!
 20!
^ E2        Form=C2*D2
Width: 9  Memory: 38 Last Col/Row:F17
  1>
```

Figure 2.9c

```
  |  A  ||    B    ||    C    ||    D    ||   E   ||   F   ||   G   |
 1|                  Output - p   Time - t   p * t       t^2
 2|1978 1st Quarter   19         -7           -133        49
 3|1978 2nd Quarter   13         -6            -78        36
 4|1978 3rd Quarter   9          -5            -45        25
 5|1978 4th Quarter   18         -4            -72        16
 6|1979 1st Quarter   22         -3            -66         9
 7|1979 2nd Quarter   15         -2            -30         4
 8|1979 3rd Quarter   14         -1            -14         1
 9|1979 4th Quarter   23          0              0         0
10|1980 1st Quarter   27          1             27         1
11|1980 2nd Quarter   17          2             34         4
12|1980 3rd Quarter   16          3             48         9
13|1980 4th Quarter   27          4            108        16
14|1981 1st Quarter   31          5            155        25
15|1981 2nd Quarter   20          6            120        36
16|1981 3rd Quarter   19          7            133        49
17|1981 4th Quarter   27          8            216        64
18|
19|                  315          8            403       344
20|
v C19         Form=SUM(C2:C17)
Width: 9  Memory: 38 Last Col/Row:F19
 1>
```

Figure 2.9d

operation falls into two parts. The first of these is covered in Chapter 4 where some of SuperCalc3's arithmetic functions are used to calculate the equation for the regression line. In Chapter 7, all the data are displayed in graphical form.

3 Formatting

Example 1 — part 2

Example 1 — The cashflow spreadsheet — part 2

Protection

Since much time and effort is devoted to setting up not only the formulae and the general contents of your spreadsheet, not to mention the formats which you define in order to improve its legibility, it is generally good practice to make sure that your efforts do not become sabotaged by the inadvertent depression of the wrong key. You can protect one or more cells from erasure by using the Protect, /P, command. This is shown in Fig. 3.1a. Here the block of cells with E16 at the top left to J21 at the bottom right are about to be protected. They will show up on the screen to be of a lower brightness than the unprotected cells and if the cursor is moved to one of these you will not be allowed to replace its contents with anything else. The same was done for the block E10:J13, the column D24:D27 and the block E23:J27. Naturally, protection is only applied after the corrected formulae have been entered and the whole spreadsheet tested. If you wish to lift protection, then the /U, Uprotect, is used

```
    :  B   ::        C          ::  D   ::   E   ::   F   ::   G   :
  1:ds)                                     A.B.C.Computers Ltd
  2:
  3:
  4:                                   1985     1986     1987     1988
  5:                               ------------------------------------
  6:                                  12500    14375    17250    22425
  7:                                             .15      .20      .30
  8:
  9:
 10: .19     of Revenue                      2731.25   3277.5  4260.75
 11: .15     of Revenue                      2156.25   2587.5  3363.75
 12: .2      of Wages                         546.25    655.5   852.15
 13: .07     Growth rate                         115   123.05 131.6635
 14:
 15:
 16: .08     of Revenue                         1150     1380     1794
 17: .1      Growth rate                        1200     1320     1452
 18: .2      of total salaries                   470      540    649.2
 19: .35     of Revenue                      5031.25   6037.5  7848.75
 20:         Fixed Annual amount                  20       20       20
^ C10         Text="of Revenue
Enter Range
 17>/Protect,e16:j21
```

Figure 3.1a

and you can answer ALL to the question asking for the range of cells to be unprotected.

User-defined formats

When the /F, Format, command is issued, the selection of formats offered are identified by

(I,G,E,£,R,L,TR,TL,*,U(1–8),H,D)

where:

I specifies an Integer (whole numbers only) format for the display.
G specifies a General format so that if a very large or a very small number is entered, then it is presented in such a way as to be displayed in 'exponential' format — 66666e10 for example, where the **e** stands for 'times 10 to the power of'. Numbers containing a number of characters less than or equal to the width of the cell will be displayed as they are entered.
E specifies that the number entered will be forced to be displayed in exponential format.
£ specifies that the number will be displayed in decimal currency format — to two places of decimals.
R and L specify that numbers will be ranged either to the (R)ight or the (L)eft of the cell.

TR and TL specify that text will be ranged either to the right or left of the cell.
* specifies that the number will be converted to an integer (whole number) and one * character is displayed for each unit in that integer. It thus produces a very elementary form of graph.
U(1–8) are the user-defined formats, of which there are eight, which are available. Their use is covered in the next section.
H enables you to hide the contents of one or more cells.
D enables you to define your own formats.

If you load your cashflow spreadsheet and press /F followed by d, for define, you will be presented with a display as shown in Fig. 3.2a. The options open to you are:

Floating £ which places a £ sign at the front of an entry.
Embedded commas which places commas in every third position reading from the left of the decimal point.
Minus in ( ) which encloses negative numbers in brackets, the way that accountants like to do it.
Zero as blank will not display entries which are zero.
% will multiply the contents of the cell by 100 and display the number followed by a % sign, i.e. 0.67 will appear as 67%.
Decimal Places will define the number of decimal places to be displayed.

```
                         User-defined formats
                         1  2  3  4  5  6  7  8
Floating  £              Y  Y  Y  Y  Y  Y  Y  Y

Embedded commas          Y  Y  Y  Y  Y  Y  Y  Y

Minus in ( )             N  N  N  N  N  N  N  N

Zero as blank            N  N  N  N  N  N  N  N

%                        N  N  N  N  N  N  N  N

Decimal Places           2  2  2  2  2  2  2  2

Scaling factor           0  0  0  0  0  0  0  0

CANCEL  to return to worksheet

^ A1           Text="PROJECTED CASH FLOW - (Thousands)
Y(es) or N(o)
 15>/Format,define
```

Figure 3.2a

```
                         User-defined formats
                         1  2  3  4  5  6  7  8
Floating  £              N  Y  Y  Y  Y  Y  Y  Y

Embedded commas          Y  Y  Y  Y  Y  Y  Y  Y

Minus in ( )             N  Y  N  N  N  N  N  N

Zero as blank            N  Y  N  N  N  N  N  N

%                        Y  N  N  N  N  N  N  N

Decimal Places           2  2  2  2  2  2  2  2

Scaling factor           0  0  0  0  0  0  0  0


CANCEL  to return to worksheet


^ A1            Text="PROJECTED CASH FLOW - (Thousands)
Y(es) or N(o)
 15>/Format,define
```

Figure 3.2b

Scaling factor will divide the number by 10 raised to the power selected before it is displayed. This means that if a scaling factor of 3 is selected, then the number is divided by 10 raised to the power of 3, 1000, and then displayed.

All you have to do is to position the cursor in the appropriate line in any of the columns and either answer (Y)es or (N)o for those which have a Y/N option, or enter

```
   :            A            ::    B    ::           C           ::     D     :
  1:PROJECTED CASH FLOW - (Thousands)
  2:
  3:
  4:YEARS:                                                                 1985
  5:                                                                 ----------
  6:Revenue                                                               12500
  7:% growth
  8:
  9:PRODUCTION COSTS
 10:Wages                            .19      of Revenue
 11:Materials                        .15      of Revenue
 12:N.I. and Pensions                .2       of Wages
 13:Packaging & Miscellaneous        .07      Growth rate
 14:
 15:SALES & OFFICE EXPENSES
 16:Marketing staff salaries         .08      of Revenue
 17:Office staff salaries            .1       Growth rate
 18:N.I. & Pensions                  .2       of total salaries
 19:Advertising                      .35      of Revenue
 20:Depreciation                              Fixed Annual amount
^A1          Text="PROJECT CASH FLOW - (Thousands)
Defined Formats: (I,G,E,£,R,L.TR,TL,*,U(1-8),H,D)
 42>/Format,Entry,b10:b13,User-defined1,Left,
```

Figure 3.3a

```
  :            A             ::   B   ::         C          ::    D    :
 1:PROJECTED CASH FLOW - (Thousands)
 2:
 3:
 4:YEARS:                                                            1985
 5:                                                             ---------
 6:Revenue                                                      >>>>>>>>
 7:% growth
 8:
 9:PRODUCTION COSTS
10:Wages                           19.00%   of Revenue
11:Materials                       15.00%   of Revenue
12:N.I. and Pensions               20.00%   of Wages
13:Packaging & Miscellaneous       7.00%    Growth rate
14:
15:SALES & OFFICE EXPENSES
16:Marketing staff salaries        8.00%    of Revenue
17:Office staff salaries           10.00%   Growth rate
18:N.I. & Pensions                 20.00%   of total salaries
19:Advertising                     35.00%   of Revenue
20:Depreciation                             Fixed Annual amount
> D6    2     Form=12500
Width: 9  Memory: 37 Last Row/Col:J27     ? for Help
  1>
```

Figure 3.4a

the appropriate number for the two numerical options. To return to the spreadsheet, you press **CANCEL** which is the first microscreen touch-sensitive key for Apricot machines and F2 on IBM PCs.

Figure 3.2b shows the table after the first two user-defined formats have been altered. Then having returned to the sheet function U1, and left justification of the numbers in the range B10:B13 have been chosen, as shown in Fig. 3.3a. Then the same format was chosen for the entries in the column B16:B19. The second user-defined format was chosen for all the numerical entries relating to money with the intention of displaying them in currency format with a floating £ sign, commas every three places and negative amounts enclosed in brackets. The result is shown in Fig. 3.4a. Note how the entry in cell D6 appears as 〉〉〉〉〉〉〉〉 which tells you that the display is too large to appear in the space allotted to it. This means a change in the width of all the columns from D to J. The final display of the complete spreadsheet is shown in Fig. 3.5. Note the result which is shown in Fig. 3.6 if the number in D6 is made much smaller.

	A	B	C	D	E	F	G	H	I	J
1	PROJECTED CASH FLOW - (Thousands)				A.B.C.Computers Ltd					
2										
3										
4	YEARS:			1985	1986	1987	1988	1989	1990	1991
5										
6	Revenue			£12,500.00	£14,375.00	£17,250.00	£22,425.00	£25,788.75	£28,367.63	£31,204.39
7	% growth				15.00%	20.00%	30.00%	15.00%	10.00%	10.00%
8										
9	PRODUCTION COSTS									
10	Wages	19.00%	of Revenue		£2,731.25	£3,277.50	£4,260.75	£4,899.86	£5,389.85	£5,928.83
11	Materials	15.00%	of Revenue		£2,156.25	£2,587.50	£3,363.75	£3,868.31	£4,255.14	£4,680.66
12	N.I. and Pensions	20.00%	of Wages		£546.25	£655.50	£852.15	£979.97	£1,077.97	£1,185.77
13	Packaging & Miscellaneous	7.00%	Growth rate		£115.00	£123.05	£131.66	£140.88	£150.74	£161.29
14										
15	SALES & OFFICE EXPENSES									
16	Marketing staff salaries	8.00%	of Revenue		£1,150.00	£1,380.00	£1,794.00	£2,063.10	£2,269.41	£2,496.35
17	Office staff salaries	10.00%	Growth rate		£1,200.00	£1,320.00	£1,452.00	£1,597.20	£1,756.92	£1,932.61
18	N.I. & Pensions	20.00%	of total salaries		£470.00	£540.00	£649.20	£732.06	£805.27	£885.79
19	Advertising	35.00%	of Revenue		£5,031.25	£6,037.50	£7,848.75	£9,026.06	£9,928.67	£10,921.54
20	Depreciation		Fixed Annual amount		£20.00	£20.00	£20.00	£20.00	£20.00	£20.00
21	Miscellaneous	£19	Annual fixed increase		£19.00	£38.00	£57.00	£76.00	£95.00	£114.00
22										
23	Total operating expenses			£6,400.00	£9,557.75	£11,321.55	£14,374.51	£16,440.49	£18,089.71	£19,901.66
24	Interest repayable	Fixed Annual amount		£13.00	£13.00	£13.00	£13.00	£13.00	£13.00	£13.00
25	Pre-Tax income			£6,087.00	£4,804.25	£5,915.45	£8,037.49	£9,335.26	£10,264.92	£11,289.73
26	Tax	48.00%	of Pre-Tax Income	£2,921.76	£2,306.04	£2,839.42	£3,857.99	£4,480.93	£4,927.16	£5,419.07
27	Net income			£3,165.24	£2,498.21	£3,076.03	£4,179.49	£4,854.34	£5,337.76	£5,870.66

Figure 3.5

	A	B	C	D	E	F	G	H	I	J
1	PROJECTED CASH FLOW - (Thousands)				A.B.C.Computers Ltd					
2										
3										
4	YEARS:			1985	1986	1987	1988	1989	1990	1991
5										
6	Revenue			£1,000.00	£1,150.00	£1,380.00	£1,794.00	£2,063.10	£2,269.41	£2,496.35
7	% growth				15.00%	20.00%	30.00%	15.00%	10.00%	10.00%
8										
9	PRODUCTION COSTS									
10	Wages	19.00%	of Revenue		£218.50	£262.20	£340.86	£391.99	£431.19	£474.31
11	Materials	15.00%	of Revenue		£172.50	£207.00	£269.10	£309.47	£340.41	£374.45
12	N.I. and Pensions	20.00%	of Wages		£43.70	£52.44	£68.17	£78.40	£86.24	£94.86
13	Packaging & Miscellaneous	7.00%	Growth rate		£115.00	£123.05	£131.66	£140.88	£150.74	£161.29
14										
15	SALES & OFFICE EXPENSES									
16	Marketing staff salaries	8.00%	of Revenue		£92.00	£110.40	£143.52	£165.05	£181.55	£199.71
17	Office staff salaries	10.00%	Growth rate		£1,200.00	£1,320.00	£1,452.00	£1,597.20	£1,756.92	£1,932.61
18	N.I. & Pensions	20.00%	of total salaries		£258.40	£286.08	£319.10	£352.45	£387.69	£426.46
19	Advertising	35.00%	of Revenue		£402.50	£483.00	£627.90	£722.09	£794.29	£873.72
20	Depreciation		Fixed Annual amount		£20.00	£20.00	£20.00	£20.00	£20.00	£20.00
21	Miscellaneous	£19	Annual fixed increase		£19.00	£19.00	£19.00	£19.00	£19.00	£19.00
22										
23	Total operating expenses			£6,400.00	£2,231.10	£2,510.57	£2,906.94	£3,239.48	£3,555.30	£3,902.41
24	Interest repayable	Fixed Annual amount		£13.00	£13.00	£13.00	£13.00	£13.00	£13.00	£13.00
25	Pre-Tax income			(£5,413.00)	(£1,094.10)	(£1,143.57)	(£1,125.94)	(£1,189.38)	(£1,298.89)	(£1,419.06)
26	Tax	48.00%	of Pre-Tax Income	(£2,598.24)	(£525.17)	(£548.91)	(£540.45)	(£570.90)	(£623.47)	(£681.15)
27	Net income			(£2,814.76)	(£568.93)	(£594.66)	(£585.49)	(£618.48)	(£675.42)	(£737.91)

Figure 3.6

4 Devising spreadsheets using SuperCalc3 arithmetic and logical functions

Example 2 — part 2; Example 3 — part 1; IF, AND, OR, NOT

Example 2 — A time series — part 2

So far in the time series example, you have arrived at the stage where you have calculated the totals of output, time (measured from an assumed mean), the product of time and output and the square of the time, and have used the SuperCalc3 SUM function to do these calculations for you. You should remember that SUM(C2:C17) means the sum of all the entries in the range C2 to C17 — the section of column C between, and including, the entries in rows 2 to 17. This is exactly the same as writing

C2 + C3 + C4 + C5 + C6 = C7 + C8 + C9
+ C10 + C11 + C12 + C13 + C14 + C15 + C16 + C17

You can also write, for example,

SUM(C2,C4,C6,C8)

which is the same as

C2 + C4 + C6 + C8

and you can write

SUM(C2 ^ 2,C5 ^ 3,C4/2)

so that you instruct SuperCalc3 to perform other arithmetic operations as it does the summing.

The current stage of the time series was shown in Fig. 2.9d and the next step is to calculate the equation of the straight line which relates **p** and **t** together. This equation is called a **linear regression** equation and has the form

$$p = a + bt$$

The value of **b** is found from the standard formula

$$\frac{\Sigma pt - (\Sigma p)(\Sigma t)/n}{\Sigma t^2 - (\Sigma t)^2/n}$$

The value of **a** is found from the standard formula

$$\frac{\Sigma p - b\Sigma t}{n}$$

so that B34 contains the formula

(E19 – (C19*D19)/16)/(F19 – ((D19 ^ 2)/16))

for **b** and B35 contains

(C19 – (B34*D19))/16

for **a**. By doing this you have obtained the equation of the straight line where the sum of the squares of the distances of the observed values from the straight line is a minimum. This is the method of 'least squares'. The result is shown in Fig. 4.1.

The time series is going to be used to forecast future production on the basis that the general trend of production has been established and that will be used to predict what the production is likely to be. The 'trend' values are found by substituting the values of **t** in the newly-calculated equation to produce the entries in column G. You will then replicate this formula down the column. This is shown in Fig. 4.2a. The final result for this part is shown in Fig. 4.2b.

```
   ¦   A   ¦¦    B    ¦¦    C    ¦¦    D    ¦¦   E   ¦¦    F   ¦
  1¦                   Output - p   Time - t   p * t       t^2
  2¦1978 1st Quarter           19         -7    -133        49
  3¦1978 2nd Quarter           13         -6     -78        36
  4¦1978 3rd Quarter            9         -5     -45        25
  5¦1978 4th Quarter           18         -4     -72        16
  6¦1979 1st Quarter           22         -3     -66         9
  7¦1979 2nd Quarter           15         -2     -30         4
  8¦1979 3rd Quarter           14         -1     -14         1
  9¦1979 4th Quarter           23          0       0         0
 10¦1980 1st Quarter           27          1      27         1
 11¦1980 2nd Quarter           17          2      34         4
 12¦1980 3rd Quarter           16          3      48         9
 13¦1980 4th Quarter           27          4     108        16
 14¦1981 1st Quarter           31          5     155        25
 15¦1981 2nd Quarter           20          6     120        36
 16¦1981 3rd Quarter           19          7     133        49
 17¦1981 4th Quarter           27          8     216        64
 18¦
 19¦                          317          8     403       344
 20¦
 21¦                    Median Values       Corrected Median
 22¦         1st Quarter
 23¦         2nd Quarter
 24¦         3rd Quarter
 25¦         4th Quarter
 26¦
 27¦
 28¦Predicted Outputs 1982
 29¦         1st Quarter
 30¦         2nd Quarter
 31¦         3rd Quarter
 32¦         4th Quarter
 33¦
 34¦b =        .719117647
 35¦a =        19.4529412
```

Figure 4.1

```
   ¦    C    ¦¦    D    ¦¦   E   ¦¦   F   ¦¦    G    ¦¦    H    ¦¦    I
  1¦ Output - p   Time - t   p * t      t^2  T (Trend)
  2¦        19          -7    -133       49 14.4191176
  3¦        13          -6     -78       36
  4¦         9          -5     -45       25
  5¦        18          -4     -72       16
  6¦        22          -3     -66        9
  7¦        15          -2     -30        4
  8¦        14          -1     -14        1
  9¦        23           0       0        0
 10¦        27           1      27        1
 11¦        17           2      34        4
 12¦        16           3      48        9
 13¦        27           4     108       16
 14¦        31           5     155       25
 15¦        20           6     120       36
 16¦        19           7     133       49
 17¦        27           8     216       64
 18¦
 19¦       317           8     403      344
 20¦
^ G2          Form=B35+B34*D2
N(o Adjust), A(sk for Adjust), V(alues), +, -, *, /
 22>/Replicate,G2,g3:g17,
```

Figure 4.2a

	C	D	E	F	G	H	I
1	Output - p	Time - t	p * t	t^2	T (Trend)		
2	19	-7	-133	49	14.4191176		
3	13	-6	-78	36	15.1382353		
4	9	-5	-45	25	15.8573529		
5	18	-4	-72	16	16.5764706		
6	22	-3	-66	9	17.2955882		
7	15	-2	-30	4	18.0147059		
8	14	-1	-14	1	18.7338235		
9	23	0	0	0	19.4529412		
10	27	1	27	1	20.1720588		
11	17	2	34	4	20.8911765		
12	16	3	48	9	21.6102941		
13	27	4	108	16	22.3294118		
14	31	5	155	25	23.0485294		
15	20	6	120	36	23.7676471		
16	19	7	133	49	24.4867647		
17	27	8	216	64	25.2058824		
18							
19	317	8	403	344			
20							

```
^ G2          Form=B35+B34*D2
Width:11   Memory: 31 Last Col/Row:G35      ? for HELP
  1>
```

Figure 4.2b

There is a standard notation for producing a 'model' of a time series. For the purpose of this example, use the formula

$$p = T + S + R$$

in which the observed value of the production is **p**, **T** is the trend, **S** is the seasonal variation and **R** represents the residual variation. (A full explanation of the theories and the

	C	D	E	F	G	H	I
1	Output - p	Time - t	p * t	t^2	T (Trend)	S + R	
2	19	-7	-133	49	14.4191176	4.580882	
3	13	-6	-78	36	15.1382353	-2.13824	
4	9	-5	-45	25	15.8573529	-6.85735	
5	18	-4	-72	16	16.5764706	1.423529	
6	22	-3	-66	9	17.2955882	4.704412	
7	15	-2	-30	4	18.0147059	-3.01471	
8	14	-1	-14	1	18.7338235	-4.73382	
9	23	0	0	0	19.4529412	3.547059	
10	27	1	27	1	20.1720588	6.827941	
11	17	2	34	4	20.8911765	-3.89118	
12	16	3	48	9	21.6102941	-5.61029	
13	27	4	108	16	22.3294118	4.670588	
14	31	5	155	25	23.0485294	7.951471	
15	20	6	120	36	23.7676471	-3.76765	
16	19	7	133	49	24.4867647	-5.48676	
17	27	8	216	64	25.2058824	1.794118	
18							
19	317	8	403	344			
20							

```
^ H2          Form=C2-G2
Width:9   Memory: 31 Last Col/Row:G35      ? for HELP
  1>
```

Figure 4.2c

mathematics of this example will be found in most standard text-books on statistics.)

From the formula, for which you already know **p** and **T**, you can write that

p − T = S + R

so that you can now produce a new column headed S + R, which is shown in Fig. 4.2c.

Next you have to find the S, or seasonal, value of the output by finding the median value of the S + R column for each of the four quarters. The median is defined as the central value of a list of numbers arranged in ascending order. If there is an even number of entries in the list, then the median is found by calculating the average of the two central values. In this case you can find the median by summing the four numbers and then subtracting the largest and the smallest, MAX and MIN, functions in SuperCalc3. The actual median is found by dividing the final answer to this calculation by two. The result is shown in Fig. 4.2d.

Under the four median values, place their average, and the method is then to place a corrected median value beside each of them. Each corrected value is found by subtracting the average from each of the medians in turn. This is just about to be done in Fig. 4.2e.

```
  :   A   ::    B    ::    C    ::    D    ::    E   ::    F    ::    G    :
 8:1979 3rd Quarter            14        -1       -14         1 18.733235
 9:1979 4th Quarter            23         0         0         0 19.4529412
10:1980 1st Quarter            27         1        27         1 20.1720588
11:1980 2nd Quarter            17         2        34         4 20.8911765
12:1980 3rd Quarter            16         3        48         9 21.6102941
13:1980 4th Quarter            27         4       108        16 22.3294118
14:1981 1st Quarter            31         5       155        25 23.0485294
15:1981 2nd Quarter            20         6       120        36 23.7676471
16:1981 3rd Quarter            19         7       133        49 24.4867647
17:1981 4th Quarter            27         8       216        64 25.2058824
18:
19:                           317         8       403       344
20:
21:                  Median Values          Corrected Median
22:          1st Quarter 5.76617647
23:          2nd Quarter -3.3911765
24:          3rd Quarter -5.5485294
25:          4th Quarter 2.67058824
26:
27:
v C25        Form=(SUM(H5,H9,H13,H17)-MAX(H5,H9,H13,H17)-MIN(H5,H9,H13,H17))/2
Width:  11  Memory:38  Last Col/Row:H35       ? for HELP
  1>
```

Figure 4.2d

```
   :   A   ::    B     ::     C    ::    D     ::    E    ::    F    ::     G     :
  8:1979 3rd Quarter            14          -1        -14          1 18.733235
  9:1979 4th Quarter            23           0          0          0 19.4529412
 10:1980 1st Quarter            27           1         27          1 20.1720588
 11:1980 2nd Quarter            17           2         34          4 20.8911765
 12:1980 3rd Quarter            16           3         48          9 21.6102941
 13:1980 4th Quarter            27           4        108         16 22.3294118
 14:1981 1st Quarter            31           5        155         25 23.0485294
 15:1981 2nd Quarter            20           6        120         36 23.7676471
 16:1981 3rd Quarter            19           7        133         49 24.4867647
 17:1981 4th Quarter            27           8        216         64 25.2058824
 18:
 19:                           317           8        403        344
 20:
 21:                 Median Values          Corrected Median
 22:         1st Quarter 5.76617647          5.891912
 23:         2nd Quarter -3.3911765
 24:         3rd Quarter -5.5485294
 25:         4th Quarter 2.67058824
 26:                     -.12573529
 27:
^ E22          Form=C22-C26
N(o Adjust), A(sk for Adjust), V(alues), +, -, *, /
  24>/Replicate,E22,e23:e25,
```

Figure 4.2e

Finally, the predicted outputs for the four quarters of the next year are found by substituting 9, 10, 11 and 12 in turn into the

$$p = a + bt$$

formula and adding these figures to each corrected median. This is shown in Fig. 4.2f. The formula used, you should

```
   :   A   ::    B     ::     C    ::    D     ::    E    ::    F    ::     G     :
 14:1981 1st Quarter            31           5        155         25 23.0485294
 15:1981 2nd Quarter            20           6        120         36 23.7676471
 16:1981 3rd Quarter            19           7        133         49 24.4867647
 17:1981 4th Quarter            27           8        216         64 25.2058824
 18:
 19:                           317           8        403        344
 20:
 21:                 Median Values          Corrected Median
 22:         1st Quarter 5.76617647          5.891912
 23:         2nd Quarter -3.3911765          -3.26544
 24:         3rd Quarter -5.5485294          -5.42279
 25:         4th Quarter 2.67058824          2.796324
 26:                     -.12573529
 27:
 28:Predicted Outputs 1982
 29:         1st Quarter 31.8169118
 30:         2nd Quarter 23.3786765
 31:         3rd Quarter 21.9404412
 32:         4th Quarter 30.8786765
 33:
v C32          Form=E25+B35+B34*(D17+4)
Width: 11  Memory: 30 Last Col/Row:H35    ? for HELP
  1>
```

Figure 4.2f

	A	B	C	D	E	F	G	H
1			Output - p	Time - t	p * t	t^2	T (Trend)	S + R
2	1978 1st Quarter		19	-7	-133	49	14.4191176	4.580882
3	1978 2nd Quarter		13	-6	-78	36	15.1382353	-2.13824
4	1978 3rd Quarter		9	-5	-45	25	15.8573529	-6.85735
5	1978 4th Quarter		18	-4	-72	16	16.5764706	1.423529
6	1979 1st Quarter		22	-3	-66	9	17.2955882	4.704412
7	1979 2nd Quarter		15	-2	-30	4	18.0147059	-3.01471
8	1979 3rd Quarter		14	-1	-14	1	18.7338235	-4.73382
9	1979 4th Quarter		23	0	0	0	19.4529412	3.547059
10	1980 1st Quarter		27	1	27	1	20.1720588	6.827941
11	1980 2nd Quarter		17	2	34	4	20.8911765	-3.89118
12	1980 3rd Quarter		16	3	48	9	21.6102941	-5.61029
13	1980 4th Quarter		27	4	108	16	22.3294118	4.670588
14	1981 1st Quarter		31	5	155	25	23.0485294	7.951471
15	1981 2nd Quarter		20	6	120	36	23.7676471	-3.76765
16	1981 3rd Quarter		19	7	133	49	24.4867647	-5.48676
17	1981 4th Quarter		27	8	216	64	25.2058824	1.794118
18							25.925	
19			317	8	403	344	26.6441176	
20							27.3632353	
21			Median Values		Corrected Median		28.0823529	
22		1st Quarter	5.76617647		5.891912			
23		2nd Quarter	-3.3911765		-3.26544			
24		3rd Quarter	-5.5485294		-5.42279			
25		4th Quarter	2.67058824		2.796324			
26			-.12573529					
27								
28	Predicted Outputs 1982							
29		1st Quarter	31.8169118					
30		2nd Quarter	23.3786765					
31		3rd Quarter	21.9404412					
32		4th Quarter	30.8786765					
33								
34	b =	.719117647						
35	a =	19.4529412						

Figure 4.3

note, is not simple to replicate since it requires first 1, then 2, then 3 and finally 4 to be added onto the number stored in D17. The easiest way to do this is to enter the formula into C29 and then replicate it into the next three cells, holding B17, B34 and B35 constant. Then you can edit, /E, these three cells and change the 1 into 2, 3 or 4 as required.

The complete spreadsheet is shown in Fig. 4.3. You should note that now the contents of the T (Trend) column have been increased by four members. This is because it was considered a worth-while exercise to show the trend projected into the next four quarters. It simply involved the substitution of values of **t** of D17 + 1, D17 + 2, etc. into the formula.

The graph which can be obtained from these results is described in Chapter 7.

Example 3 — Another time series — part 1

The next time series to be illustrated makes use of further SuperCalc3 arithmetic functions. Ultimately it is going to allow you to produce a graph relating the output from a factory, the number of operators on the production line, their average earnings and the average daily output of each operator.

The spreadsheet shown in Fig. 4.4 shows the contents of the various cells over the years from 1976 to 1981. The average daily output is obtained by assuming that there are 230 working days available in each year. In order to plot a graph which is both meaningful and easy to read, the natural logarithms of the four dependent variables are calculated, cells B12:E17. The values of these logarithms, only to make the graph scale less wasteful of space, are reduced by subtracting the whole number part of the smallest number in each column from the numbers in that column, cells B21:E26. The final result is shown in the spreadsheet illustrated in Fig. 4.5.

```
   !   A    !!          B          !!         C          !!          D              !!   E   !
  1!Year      Output (000s)          No. of Operators       Avg. daily output/Operator  Hourly ea
  2!
  3! 1976      501                     100                   B3*1000/230/C3              134
  4! A3+1      503                     98                    B4*1000/230/C4              144
  5! A4+1      512                     98                    B5*1000/230/C5              150
  6! A5+1      524                     96                    B6*1000/230/C6              178
  7! A6+1      545                     80                    B7*1000/230/C7              203
  8! A7+1      567                     77                    B8*1000/230/C8              215
  9!
 10!Logarithms of above values
 11!Year
 12! 1976      LOG(B3)                 LOG(C3)               LOG(D3)                     LOG(E3)
 13! A12+1     LOG(B4)                 LOG(C4)               LOG(D4)                     LOG(E4)
 14! A13+1     LOG(B5)                 LOG(C5)               LOG(D5)                     LOG(E5)
 15! A14+1     LOG(B6)                 LOG(C6)               LOG(D6)                     LOG(E6)
 16! A15+1     LOG(B7)                 LOG(C7)               LOG(D7)                     LOG(E7)
 17! A16+1     LOG(B8)                 LOG(C8)               LOG(D8)                     LOG(E8)
 18!
 19!Reduced logarithmic values
 20!Year
 21! 1976      B12-INT(MIN(B12:B17)) C12-INT(MIN(C12:C17)) D12-INT(MIN(D12:D17))       E12-INT(
 22! A21+1     B13-INT(MIN(B12:B17)) C13-INT(MIN(C12:C17)) D13-INT(MIN(D12:D17))       E13-INT(
 23! A22+1     B14-INT(MIN(B12:B17)) C14-INT(MIN(C12:C17)) D14-INT(MIN(D12:D17))       E14-INT(
 24! A23+1     B15-INT(MIN(B12:B17)) C15-INT(MIN(C12:C17)) D15-INT(MIN(D12:D17))       E15-INT(
 25! A24+1     B16-INT(MIN(B12:B17)) C16-INT(MIN(C12:C17)) D16-INT(MIN(D12:D17))       E16-INT(
 26! A25+1     B17-INT(MIN(B12:B17)) C17-INT(MIN(C12:C17)) D17-INT(MIN(D12:D17))       E17-INT(
```

Figure 4.4

	A	B	C	D	E
1	Year	Output (000s)	No. of Operators	Avg. daily output/Operator	Hourly ea
2					
3	1976	501	100	21.78	134
4	1977	503	98	22.32	144
5	1978	512	98	22.72	150
6	1979	524	96	23.73	178
7	1980	545	80	29.62	203
8	1981	567	77	32.02	215
9					
10	Logarithms of above values				
11	Year				
12	1976	2.70	2.00	1.34	2.13
13	1977	2.70	1.99	1.35	2.16
14	1978	2.71	1.99	1.36	2.18
15	1979	2.72	1.98	1.38	2.25
16	1980	2.74	1.90	1.47	2.31
17	1981	2.75	1.89	1.51	2.33
18					
19	Reduced logarithmic values				
20	Year				
21	1976	.70	1.00	.34	.13
22	1977	.70	.99	.35	.16
23	1978	.71	.99	.36	.18
24	1979	.72	.98	.38	.25
25	1980	.74	.90	.47	.31
26	1981	.75	.89	.51	.33

Figure 4.5

IF, AND, OR, NOT

SuperCalc3 has the ability to examine the truth or otherwise of an expression and record this either as FALSE, displayed as 0, or TRUE, displayed as 1. An expression is deemed to be TRUE if it evaluates to a non-zero number and FALSE if it evaluates to zero. This enables you to allow SuperCalc3 to make a decision, based on the contents of a specified cell, about what should be placed in another cell. For example, if you want to perform a calculation if and only if a certain condition is fulfilled, then you can do it by using

IF(Condition,form1,form2)

so that

IF(A2 = A4,0,100)

means that if the contents of cells A2 and A4 are the same, then the current cell displays a zero. If not, then 100 is displayed. An example of this is shown which calculates various rates of discount. If the number of items purchased, entered into B1, is less than 10, then no discount is allowed. If there are 10 or more, but less than 100, then a 10 per cent discount is allowed. If 100 or more but less than 250, then 30 per cent discount is given; 250 or more items purchased give you a 40 per cent discount. This is achieved by 'nesting' the IF statements. The spreadsheet showing the display is shown in Fig. 4.6 and the contents of the cells are listed in Fig. 4.7. This is done by choosing the C option from the /O, Output, command. The IF statements are shown in cell B6, which is formatted to display the figures as percentages by using User Format 1.

```
 |          A          ||   B   ||      C      |
1|No. of items bought      150
2|Cost per item           £1.25
3|
4|Gross cost                              £187.50
5|
6|Discount @            30.00%             £56.25
7|------------------------------------------------
8|Total bill                              £131.25
9|------------------------------------------------
```

Figure 4.6

```
SuperCalc ver.  1.00
No. of items bought
A1          = "No. of items bought
B1          = 150
A2          = "Cost per item
B2 2        = 1.25
A4          = "Gross cost
C4          = B1*B2
A6          = "Discount @
B6 1        = IF(B1<10,0,IF(B1<100,.1,IF(B1<250,.3,.4)))
C6          = C4*B6
A7          = '-
A8          = "Total bill
C8          = C4-C6
A9          = '-
```

Figure 4.7

AND is used to display a 1 if two expressions are true, that is they are both non-zero, or 0 if either one is zero. So you write

AND(Expr1,Expr2)

OR is similar in that it displays 1 if one of the two expressions is non-zero and 0 otherwise

OR(Expr1,Expr2)

An example using AND, together with IFs, is shown in Fig. 4.8. It displays whether a person is eligible for free NHS glasses on the grounds of age and weekly income. If the income is under £26 and the age is under 19 years, then the person is eligible for free glasses. The actual contents of the spreadsheet are shown in Fig. 4.9. Notice how several of the entries have been hidden from display, by choosing the H option from the /F command.

Figures 4.10 and 4.11 show the above example extended using OR as well as AND and IF to decide on eligibility for free NHS glasses if the person is either under 19 and earning less than £26 or 65 or over and earning less than £35.

```
 !   A    !!   B    !!   C   !
1!Earnings          18
2!Age               17
3!
4!Eligible for free glasses
5!                 YES
```

Figure 4.8

```
SuperCalc ver.  1.00
Earnings
A1        = "Earnings
B1        = 18
C1 H      = IF(B1<26,1,0)
A2        = "Age
B2        = 17
C2 H      = IF(B2<20,1,0)
A4        = "Eligible for free glasses
A5 H      = AND(C1,C2)
B5        = IF(A5,"YES","NO")
```

Figure 4.9

```
  |    A    ||    B    ||    C    ||    D    |
 1|Earnings          31
 2|Age               70
 3|
 4|Eligible for free glasses              YES
 5|
```

Figure 4.10

```
SuperCalc ver.  1.00
Earnings
A1        = "Earnings
B1        = 31
C1 H      = IF(B1<26,1,0)
D1 H      = IF(B1<35,1,0)
A2        = "Age
B2        = 70
C2 H      = IF(B2<19,1,0)
D2 H      = IF(B2>64,1,0)
A3        = AND(C1,C2)
B3        = AND(D1,D2)
C3        = OR(A3,B3)
A4        = "Eligible for free glasses
D4        = IF(C3=1,"YES","NO")
```

Figure 4.11

NOT will simply negate the truth value of an expression, so that if the contents of A1 are non-zero, then

NOT(A1)

will display zero and if the contents of A1 are zero, then 1 is displayed.

5 Sorting and consolidation

ARRANGE: consolidation of spreadsheets

ARRANGE

A SuperCalc3 spreadsheet can have rows or columns sorted into ascending or descending alphabetical or numerical order by use of the /A, Arrange, command. Let us consider the sheet shown in Fig. 5.1a. We are going to re-arrange the rows so that the names are in alphabetical order. You choose

```
   |       A       ||   B   ||    C    ||   D   ||   E   ||   F   ||   G   |
  1|           NAME      AGE    SALARY
  2|------------------------------------------------------------------------
  3|Smith, N.V.           45   7000.00
  4|Jones, H.N.           34   4503.00
  5|Harris, T.B.          21   7890.00
  6|Foster, J.C.          47   5450.00
  7|Johnson, H.           60   6890.00
  8|Davison, P.B.         32   4440.00
  9|Harding, G.J.         44   9000.00
 10|Wallis, G.            21   4500.00
 11|Dawson, J.J.          32   6500.00
 12|Viney, J.C.           54   7850.00
 13|Adams, P.             66  11500.00
 14|Whitwell, A.E.        37   8790.00
 15|Saunders, J.          29   6860.00
 16|Campbell, C.C.        30   8000.00
 17|MacIntyre, J.A.       18   3500.00
 18|Willis, J.            41   7000.00
 19|
 20|Average:              38   6854.56
< A1         Text="NAME"
Width: 15  Memory:41  Last Col/Row:C20      ? for HELP
  1>
```

Figure 5.1a

```
   |      A      ||   B   ||   C   ||   D   ||   E   ||   F   ||   G   |
  1|           NAME        AGE    SALARY
  2|-----------------------------------------------------------------------
  3|Smith, N.V.             45   7000.00
  4|Jones, H.N.             34   4503.00
  5|Harris, T.B.            21   7890.00
  6|Foster, J.C.            47   5450.00
  7|Johnson, H.             60   6890.00
  8|Davison, P.B.           32   4440.00
  9|Harding, G.J.           44   9000.00
 10|Wallis, G.              21   4500.00
 11|Dawson, J.J.            32   6500.00
 12|Viney, J.C.             54   7850.00
 13|Adams, P.               66  11500.00
 14|Whitwell, A.E.          37   8790.00
 15|Saunders, J.            29   6860.00
 16|Campbell, C.C.          30   8000.00
 17|MacIntyre, J.A.         18   3500.00
 18|Willis, J.              41   7000.00
 19|
 20|Average:                38   6854.56
< A1         Text="NAME"
R(ow) or C(olumn)?
 10>/Arrange,
```

Figure 5.1b

the /A command and are asked if you are to sort by row or column, shown in Fig. 5.1b. Choose the C option and you are asked for the key column, which happens to be column A. At this point you must be careful not to press RETURN unless you really mean it. This is because if you do press RETURN, the complete contents of column A will be sorted, and that includes the headings and the averages. So press the comma (,) key before pressing RETURN and this gives you

```
   |      A      ||   B   ||   C   ||   D   ||   E   ||   F   ||   G   |
  1|           NAME        AGE    SALARY
  2|-----------------------------------------------------------------------
  3|Smith, N.V.             45   7000.00
  4|Jones, H.N.             34   4503.00
  5|Harris, T.B.            21   7890.00
  6|Foster, J.C.            47   5450.00
  7|Johnson, H.             60   6890.00
  8|Davison, P.B.           32   4440.00
  9|Harding, G.J.           44   9000.00
 10|Wallis, G.              21   4500.00
 11|Dawson, J.J.            32   6500.00
 12|Viney, J.C.             54   7850.00
 13|Adams, P.               66  11500.00
 14|Whitwell, A.E.          37   8790.00
 15|Saunders, J.            29   6860.00
 16|Campbell, C.C.          30   8000.00
 17|MacIntyre, J.A.         18   3500.00
 18|Willis, J.              41   7000.00
 19|
 20|Average:                38   6854.56
< A1         Text="NAME"
Enter Row Range
 23>/Arrange,Column,a,3:18
```

Figure 5.1c

```
   !       A       !!   B   !!   C   !!   D   !!   E   !!   F   !!   G   !
 1!            NAME       AGE    SALARY
 2!-----------------------------------------------------------------------
 3!Smith, N.V.             45   7000.00
 4!Jones, H.N.             34   4503.00
 5!Harris, T.B.            21   7890.00
 6!Foster, J.C.            47   5450.00
 7!Johnson, H.             60   6890.00
 8!Davison, P.B.           32   4440.00
 9!Harding, G.J.           44   9000.00
10!Wallis, G.              21   4500.00
11!Dawson, J.J.            32   6500.00
12!Viney, J.C.             54   7850.00
13!Adams, P.               66  11500.00
14!Whitwell, A.E.          37   8790.00
15!Saunders, J.            29   6860.00
16!Campbell, C.C.          30   8000.00
17!MacIntyre, J.A.         18   3500.00
18!Willis, J.              41   7000.00
19!
20!Average:                38   6854.56
< A1          Tex="NAME"
A(scending) or D(escending) ?
 24>/Arrange,Column,a,3:18,
```

Figure 5.1d

the chance to specify the range of rows to be sorted. You should remember that all the rows across the sheet will be rearranged, and in this case you specify that rows 3 to 18 will be sorted, as shown in Fig. 5.1c. Then you are asked if the sort is to be in ascending or descending order, as shown in Fig. 5.1d. You want no adjustments to be made to any formulae — you want to maintain the calculation of the

```
   !       A       !!   B   !!   C   !!   D   !!   E   !!   F   !!   G   !
 1!            NAME       AGE    SALARY
 2!-----------------------------------------------------------------------
 3!Smith, N.V.             45   7000.00
 4!Jones, H.N.             34   4503.00
 5!Harris, T.B.            21   7890.00
 6!Foster, J.C.            47   5450.00
 7!Johnson, H.             60   6890.00
 8!Davison, P.B.           32   4440.00
 9!Harding, G.J.           44   9000.00
10!Wallis, G.              21   4500.00
11!Dawson, J.J.            32   6500.00
12!Viney, J.C.             54   7850.00
13!Adams, P.               66  11500.00
14!Whitwell, A.E.          37   8790.00
15!Saunders, J.            29   6860.00
16!Campbell, C.C.          30   8000.00
17!MacIntyre, J.A.         18   3500.00
18!Willis, J.              41   7000.00
19!
20!Average:                38   6854.56
< A1          Text="NAME"
Adjust? Y(es) or N(o): then <RETURN> or <,> for options
 35>/Arrange,Column,a,3:18,Ascending,N
```

Figure 5.1e

```
   :       A       ::   B   ::   C   ::   D   ::   E   ::   F   ::   G   :
  1:          NAME        AGE    SALARY
  2:-----------------------------------------------------------------------
  3:Adams, P.              66 11500.00
  4:Campbell, C.C.         30  8000.00
  5:Davison, P.B.          32  4440.00
  6:Dawson, J.J.           32  6500.00
  7:Foster, J.C.           47  5450.00
  8:Harding, G.J.          44  9000.00
  9:Harris, T.B.           21  7890.00
 10:Johnson, H.            60  6890.00
 11:Jones, H.N.            34  4503.00
 12:MacIntyre, J.A.        18  3500.00
 13:Saunders, J.           29  6860.00
 14:Smith, N.V.            45  7000.00
 15:Viney, J.C.            54  7850.00
 16:Wallis, G.             21  4500.00
 17:Whitwell, A.E.         37  8790.00
 18:Willis, J.             41  7000.00
 19:
 20:Average:               38  6854.56
> A1          Text="NAME"
Width:15  Memory: 41  Last Col/Row:C20      ? for HELP
```

Figure 5.1f

averages as before (as shown in Fig. 5.1e) and no options are chosen. Choosing the adjustment option at this point can produce some very strange effects. It is probably a good idea to save your unsorted spreadsheet before attempting any sort. Once sorting has taken place, you cannot backtrack. The result is shown in Fig. 5.1f.

The options offered at the end of the last example are made use of in the next spreadsheet. In this, a list of persons

```
   :     A     ::      B     ::   C   ::   D   ::   E   ::   F   ::   G   :
  1:DEPT        NAME           Salary
  2:-----------------------------------------------------------------------
  3:Planning    George, K.          4563
  4:Accounts    Harris, J.H.        6758
  5:R & D       Friedman, H.        5600
  6:Accounts    Rogers, K.          4600
  7:Personnel   Sharp, B.J.         4500
  8:Personnel   Sharp, A.J.         7900
  9:Planning    Kenning, J.         8100
 10:Accounts    Smith, H.           7800
 11:R & D       Jones, K.R.         5673
 12:R & D       Harris, G.          3450
 13:Production  Potter, F.          2900
 14:Planning    Potter, A.          9000
 15:Accounts    Tilsley, I.        10100
 16:Accounts    Tilsley, D.        14000
 17:Production  Cope, K.            7000
 18:Accounts    Vokes, A.F.         8000
 19:R & D       Jordan, R.          9500
 20:
^ A1        Text="DEPT"
Width:12  Memory: 41  Last Col/Row:C19      ? for HELP
  1>
```

Figure 5.2a

```
  :     A     ::     B     ::   C   ::   D   ::   E   ::   F   ::   G   :
 1:DEPT        NAME          Salary
 2:-----------------------------------------------------------------------
 3:Planning    George, K.       4563
 4:Accounts    Harris, J.H.     6758
 5:R & D       Friedman, H.     5600
 6:Accounts    Rogers, K.       4600
 7:Personnel   Sharp, B.J.      4500
 8:Personnel   Sharp, A.J.      7900
 9:Planning    Kenning, J.      8100
10:Accounts    Smith, H.        7800
11:R & D       Jones, K.R.      5673
12:R & D       Harris, G.       3450
13:Production  Potter, F.       2900
14:Planning    Potter, A.       9000
15:Accounts    Tilsley, I.     10100
16:Accounts    Tilsley, D.     14000
17:Production  Cope, K.         7000
18:Accounts    Vokes, A.F.      8000
19:R & D       Jordan, R.       9500
20:
^ A1          Text="DEPT"
Enter Secondary sort column
 37>/Arrange,Column,a:3:19,N,b
```

Figure 5.2b

working in a range of departments are to be sorted not only into departments but into an alphabetical list of names within each department (see Fig. 5.2a). The sort proceeds in exactly the same way as the first example, but when the options are offered you accept them and have the chance of specifying a secondary sort column so that you can sort names within departments, Fig. 5.2b, with the result shown in Fig. 5.2c.

```
  :     A     ::     B     ::   C   ::   D   ::   E   ::   F   ::   G   :
 1:DEPT        NAME          Salary
 2:-----------------------------------------------------------------------
 3:Accounts    Harris, J.H.     6758
 4:Accounts    Rogers, K.       4600
 5:Accounts    Smith, H.        7800
 6:Accounts    Tilsley, D.     14000
 7:Accounts    Tilsley, I.     10100
 8:Accounts    Vokes, A.F.      8000
 9:Personnel   Sharp, A.J.      7900
10:Personnel   Sharp, B.J.      4500
11:Planning    George, K.       4563
12:Planning    Kenning, J.      8100
13:Planning    Potter, A.       9000
14:Production  Cope, K.         7000
15:Production  Potter, F.       2900
16:R & D       Friedman, H.     5600
17:R & D       Harris, G.       3450
18:R & D       Jones, K.R.      5673
19:R & D       Jordan, R.       9500
20:
^ A1        Text="DEPT"
Width: 12 Memory: 41  Last Col/Row:C19     ? for HELP
  1>
```

Figure 5.2c

Consolidation of spreadsheets

Very often you need to be able to add the contents of one or more spreadsheets into another spreadsheet: this is known as 'consolidation'. There are several ways of doing this. The first is shown in the next example. Suppose you have three separate sheets each containing the details of one's monthly expenditure. These are shown in Figs 5.3, 5.4 and 5.5. Another sheet, empty at present, is going to be used to receive the information kept on the three separate sheets and combine it so as to produce a grand total. The empty sheet, ready to receive the information, is shown in Fig. 5.6. The formulae to calculate the grand totals are entered in cells A13 to G13. You then position the cursor in cell A3 and load that part of the sheet called JANEX which contains the data, the block of cells from A3 to G4, at the cursor position. The command is shown in Fig. 5.6a. On pressing RETURN you will see that the data has been entered and the totals updated. You then move the cursor to cell A6 and repeat this for the next sheet — this is shown in Fig. 5.6b. The final result is the consolidated spreadsheet shown in Fig. 5.7.

	A	B	C	D	E	F	G
1	Rent	Heat/Light	Gas	Food	Entertainment	Car	TOTAL
2	==========	==========	==========	==========	==========	==========	==========
3	January						
4	124.00	32.50	12.00	150.00	25.00	60.00	403.50

Figure 5.3

	A	B	C	D	E	F	G
1	Rent	Heat/Light	Gas	Food	Entertainment	Car	TOTAL
2	==========	==========	==========	==========	==========	==========	==========
3	February						
4	124.00	45.00	15.00	160.00	10.00	100.00	454.00

Figure 5.4

	A	B	C	D	E	F	G
1	Rent	Heat/Light	Gas	Food	Entertainment	Car	TOTAL
2	==========	==========	==========	==========	==========	==========	==========
3	March						
4	124.00	23.00	20.00	120.00	45.00	50.00	382.00

Figure 5.5

```
  |   A   ||      B     ||    C   ||   D   ||      E        ||   F   ||    G   |
 1|      Rent  Heat/Light       Gas      Food  Entertainment        Car     TOTAL
 2|=============================================================================
 3|
 4|
 5|
 6|
 7|
 8|
 9|
10|
11|
12|TOTAL
13|       .00          .00       .00      .00            .00        .00       .00
```

Figure 5.6

```
  |   A   ||      B     ||    C   ||   D   ||      E        ||   F   ||    G   |
 1|      Rent  Heat/Light       Gas      Food  Entertainment        Car     TOTAL
 2|=============================================================================
 3|
 4|
 5|
 6|
 7|
 8|
 9|
10|
11|
12|TOTAL
13|       .00          .00       .00      .00            .00        .00       .00
14|
15|
16|
17|
18|
19|
20|
^ A3
To? (Enter Cell); then <RETURN> or <,> for Options
 24>/Load,JANEX,Part,a3:g4,
```

Figure 5.6a

```
  |   A   ||      B     ||    C   ||   D   ||      E        ||   F   ||    G   |
 1|      Rent  Heat/Light       Gas      Food  Entertainment        Car     TOTAL
 2|=============================================================================
 3|January
 4|    124.00        32.50     12.00   150.00          25.00      60.00    403.50
 5|
 6|
 7|
 8|
 9|
10|
11|
12|TOTAL
13|    124.00        32.50     12.00   150.00          25.00      60.00    403.50
14|
15|
16|
17|
18|
19|
20|
v A6
To? (Enter Cell); then <RETURN> or <,> for Options
 24>/Load,FEBEX,Part,a3:g4,
```

Figure 5.6b

```
  :   A   ::       B      ::    C   ::    D   ::        E          ::    F   ::    G   :
 1:      Rent  Heat/Light        Gas      Food  Entertainment          Car     TOTAL
 2:=====================================================================================
 3:January
 4:    124.00        32.50     12.00   150.00            25.00     60.00    403.50
 5:
 6:February
 7:    124.00        45.00     15.00   160.00            10.00    100.00    454.00
 8:
 9:March
10:    124.00        23.00     20.00   120.00            45.00     50.00    382.00
11:
12:TOTAL
13:    372.00       100.50     47.00   430.00            80.00    210.00   1239.50
```

Figure 5.7

Another way of consolidating spreadsheets is to load the first one, JANEX in this case, and then load the next one, FEBEX, on top of it but specify that you are going to load PART of that sheet and state that that part is in fact ALL of the sheet. The options you are now given are to add, subtract, multiply or divide the corresponding entries. In this example, shown in Fig. 5.8a, opt to add the entries from the source sheet onto the corresponding entries of the target sheet, which will produce the result shown in Fig. 5.8b. Notice that only the numbers have been affected; the text entries are unchanged, hence the name of the month is unaltered.

```
  :   A   ::       B      ::    C   ::    D   ::        E          ::    F   ::    G   :
 1:      Rent  Heat/Light        Gas      Food  Entertainment          Car     TOTAL
 2:=====================================================================================
 3:January
 4:    124.00        32.50     12.00   150.00            25.00     60.00    403.50
 5:
 6:
 7:
 8:
 9:
10:
11:
12:
13:
14:
15:
16:
17:
18:
19:
20:
^ A1        Text="Rent"
N(o Adjust), A(sk for Adjust), V(alues), +, -, *, /
 25>/Load,FEBEX,Part,all,A1
```

Figure 5.8a

```
    :    A    ::      B     ::    C   ::  `D   ::         E          ::    F   ::    G   :
  1:      Rent  Heat/Light       Gas      Food  Entertainment          Car     TOTAL
  2:=============================================================================
  3:January
  4:    248.00          77.50     27.00   310.00              35.00   160.00    857.50
  5:
  6:
  7:
  8:
  9:
 10:
 11:
 12:
 13:
 14:
 15:
 16:
 17:
 18:
 19:
 20:
^ A1        Tex="Rent"
Width:   9   Memory: 11   Last Col/Row:G4     ? for HELP
```

Figure 5.8b

The above example produces exactly the same result as if you used the Consolidate option by entering the command

/Load,FEBEX,Consolidate

6 Windows and titles

WINDOW; TITLE

WINDOW

The WINDOW, /W, command allows you to divide your worksheet into two separate areas so that you bring sections of the sheet which are far removed from each other into close proximity. Take, for example, the cashflow sheet. If you bring it to the screen and select the /W command, as is

```
   :              A              ::   B   ::          C          ::    D     :
  1:PROJECTED CASH FLOW - (Thousands)
  2:
  3:
  4:YEARS:                                                               1985
  5:                                                              -----------
  6:Revenue                                                       £12,500.00
  7:% growth
  8:
  9:PRODUCTION COSTS
 10:Wages                          19.00%  of Revenue
 11:Materials                      15.00%  of Revenue
 12:N.I. and Pensions              20.00%  of Wages
 13:Packaging & Miscellaneous      7.00%   Growth rate
 14:
 15:SALES & OFFICE EXPENSES
 16:Marketing staff salaries       8.00%   of Revenue
 17:Office staff salaries          10.00%  Growth rate
 18:N.I. & Pensions                20.00%  of total salaries
 19:Advertising                    35.00%  of Revenue
 20:Depreciation                           Fixed Annual amount
> B1
H(oriz), V(ert), C(lear Split), S(ynch.) or U(nsynch.)
  9>/Window,
```

Figure 6.1a

```
   :            A              :      :    E    ::    F    ::    G    :
  1:PROJECTED CASH FLOW - (Thousan   1:A.B.C.Computers Ltd
  2:                                 2:
  3:                                 3:
  4:YEARS:                           4:        1986        1987        1988
  5:                                 5:------------------------------------
  6:Revenue                          6: £14,375.00  £17,250.00  £22,425.00
  7:% growth                         7:     15.00%      20.00%      30.00%
  8:                                 8:
  9:PRODUCTION COSTS                 9:
 10:Wages                           10:  £2,731.25   £3,277.50   £4,260.75
 11:Materials                       11:  £2,156.25   £2,587.50   £3,363.75
 12:N.I. and Pensions               12:    £546.25     £655.50     £852.15
 13:Packaging & Miscellaneous       13:    £115.00     £123.05     £131.66
 14:                                14:
 15:SALES & OFFICE EXPENSES         15:
 16:Marketing staff salaries        16:  £1,150.00   £1,380.00   £1,794.00
 17:Office staff salaries           17:  £1,200.00   £1,320.00   £1,452.00
 18:N.I. & Pensions                 18:    £470.00     £540.00     £649.20
 19:Advertising                     19:  £5,031.25   £6,037.50   £7,848.75
 20:Depreciation                    20:     £20.00      £20.00      £20.00
> G1
Width:12  Memory: 30  Last Col/Row:J27   ? for HELP
  1>
```

Figure 6.1b

shown in Fig. 6.1a, you can choose to divide the sheet into two independent windows, vertically split in this case, with the cursor position, B1, defining the width of the window. Each window can be moved around the screen independently of the other so that you can have the display as shown in Fig. 6.1b. Vertical scrolling can be synchronized so that as one window scrolls up, the other moves up or down by the

```
   :            A              :      :    E    ::    F    ::    G    :
 10:Wages                           10:  £2,731.25   £3,277.50   £4,260.75
 11:Materials                       11:  £2,156.25   £2,587.50   £3,363.75
 12:N.I. and Pensions               12:    £546.25     £655.50     £852.15
 13:Packaging & Miscellaneous       13:    £115.00     £123.05     £131.66
 14:                                14:
 15:SALES & OFFICE EXPENSES         15:
 16:Marketing staff salaries        16:  £1,150.00   £1,380.00   £1,794.00
 17:Office staff salaries           17:  £1,200.00   £1,320.00   £1,452.00
 18:N.I. & Pensions                 18:    £470.00     £540.00     £649.20
 19:Advertising                     19:  £5,031.25   £6,037.50   £7,848.75
 20:Depreciation                    20:     £20.00      £20.00      £20.00
 21:Miscellaneous                   21:     £19.00      £19.00      £19.00
 22:                                22:------------------------------------
 23:Total operating expenses        23:  £9,557.75  £11,302.55  £14,336.51
 24:Interest repayable              24:     £13.00      £13.00      £13.00
 25:Pre-Tax income                  25:  £4,804.25   £5,934.45   £8,075.49
 26:Tax                             26:  £2,306.04   £2,848.54   £3,876.23
 27:Net income                      27:  £2,498.21   £3,085.91   £4,199.25
 28:
 29:
v G29
Width: 12  Memory:  30  Last Col/Row:j27    ? for HELP
  1>
```

Figure 6.1c

same amount. To move the cursor from one window to the next you press the ; key. Figure 6.1c shows how the use of this command helps you to keep track of the meaning of the numbers on the sheet by keeping the names of the various rows continually in view.

TITLE

Another way that enables you to hold sections of the sheet steady while scrolling through the rest is to use the /T, TITLE, command. This enables you to define a section, above and/or to the left of the current cursor position, which always remains stationary while the rest of the sheet moves inside it. This is extremely useful for keeping track of information stored in a very large sheet. In the example shown in Fig. 6.1d, the cursor was placed at cell A5, TITLE command was selected and from the

H(oriz.), V(ert.), B(oth), C(lear)

options the **B** option was taken. This enables you to move through the sheet and still know that the figure of £732.06 referred to NI and Pensions in 1989.

You can, of course, have a window and fixed titles if you

```
    |             A              ||      G      ||      H      ||      I      |
   1|PROJECTED CASH FLOW - (Thousan
   2|
   3|
   4|YEARS:                                  1988          1989          1990
   5|                              ------------------------------------------
  15|SALES & OFFICE EXPENSES
  16|Marketing staff salaries          £1,794.00     £2,063.10     £2,269.41
  17|Office staff salaries             £1,452.00     £1,597.20     £1,756.92
  18|N.I. & Pensions                     £649.20       £732.06       £805.27
  19|Advertising                       £7,848.75     £9,026.06     £9,928.67
  20|Depreciation                         £20.00        £20.00        £20.00
  21|Miscellaneous                        £19.00        £19.00        £19.00
  22|                              ------------------------------------------
  23|Total operating expenses         £14,336.51    £16,383.49    £18,013.71
  24|Interest repayable                   £13.00        £13.00        £13.00
  25|Pre-Tax income                    £8,075.49     £9,392.26    £10,340.92
  26|Tax                               £3,876.23     £4,508.29     £4,963.64
  27|Net income                        £4,199.25     £4,883.98     £5,377.28
  28|
  29|
 < G29
Width: 12  Memory: 30 Last Col/Row:J27       ? for HELP
   1>
```

Figure 6.1d

```
    :         A          ::    :     H      ::     I      ::     J      :
  1:PROJECTED CASH FLOW - (Thousan   1:
  2:                                 2:
  3:                                 3:
  4:YEARS:                           4:        1989        1990        1991
  5:                                 5:------------------------------------
 16:Marketing staff salaries        16:   £2,063.10   £2,269.41   £2,496.35
 17:Office staff salaries           17:   £1,597.20   £1,756.92   £1,932.61
 18:N.I. & Pensions                 18:     £732.06     £805.27     £885.79
 19:Advertising                     19:   £9,026.06   £9,928.67  £10,921.54
 20:Depreciation                    20:      £20.00      £20.00      £20.00
 21:Miscellaneous                   21:      £19.00      £19.00      £19.00
 22:                                22:------------------------------------
 23:Total operating expenses        23:  £16,383.49  £18,013.71  £19,806.66
 24:Interest repayable              24:      £13.00      £13.00      £13.00
 25:Pre-Tax income                  25:   £9,392.26  £10,340.92  £11,384.73
 26:Tax                             26:   £4,508.29   £4,963.64   £5,464.67
 27:Net income                      27:   £4,883.98   £5,377.28   £5,920.06
 28:                                28:
 29:                                29:
 30:                                30:
v J30
Width: 12  Memory: 30 Last Col/Row:J27      ? for HELP
  1>
```

Figure 6.1e

so desire. In Fig. 6.1e you have the same spreadsheet with a vertical window as before and both vertical and horizontal titles. In addition, it is necessary to select the Synchronization option for scrolling the windows, otherwise the vertical titles would become meaningless. When the sheet is saved, the window and title information is saved as well. However, when you come to print a sheet you will find that you cannot print it in a window form. You could only do this by selecting certain sections only from the sheet to print at a time.

7 Plotting graphs

VIEW, selecting the variables, selecting the graph type, selecting the graphics parameters, viewing and plotting; Example 1 — part 3; Example 2 — part 3; Example 3 — part 2; some other graphs

VIEW, selecting the variables, selecting the graph type, selecting the graphics parameters, viewing and plotting

SuperCalc3 provides very easy access to a series of graphics commands that enable you not only to plot graphs of various types but also to view the proposed graph on the screen before committing yourself to printing the final graph. The command which allows you to define the areas of the spreadsheet to be graphed is /V, VIEW. The first example is a very simple spreadsheet showing income and expenditure. The basic information is contained in the spreadsheet shown in Fig. 7.1.

From the /V command you can choose the number of the graph, since several different ones can be drawn from the same set of data, as in Fig. 7.1a. First of all, choose a bar chart to be drawn from the G, Graph-type, option.

Then choose the data to be graphed by selecting the D option. At this point you can define the range of data for up

```
 |     A       ||     B     ||     C     ||     D     ||     E     ||     F     ||     G     |
 1|First half of 1986     All amounts in Pounds Sterling
 2|                   Jan.        Feb.        Mar.        Apr.        May.        Jun.
 3|Income          1100.00      965.00     1245.00     1543.00      875.00      985.00
 4|Expenses         450.00      567.00      982.00      560.00      700.00      854.00
 5|Amount left      650.00      398.00      263.00      983.00      175.00      131.00
```

Figure 7.1

to ten variables to be plotted on the same graph. Plot the data defined by the range of cells B3:G3 for the first variable, variable A, B4:G4 for variable B and B5:G5 for variable C. As you need to distinguish the three variables from each other, specify the labels to be attached to each of the three superimposed graphs — the variable labels are chosen from the V option and are specified as the contents of the cells A3, A4 and A5. Finally, ensure from the H option, that the contents of A1 and C1 provide the main heading and the X-axis (horizontal axis) headings. In order to see the way the graph has been set up, press the ? key while the /V command is selected. The resulting display is shown in Fig. 7.1b.

The /G, Global, command and its G, Graphics, option allow you to specify to SuperCalc3 just how you want your graphs to be displayed. The F, Fonts, option allows you to choose the type of text to be printed; the D, Device, option tells SuperCalc3 what type of printer or plotter is being used.

```
 |     A       ||     B     ||     C     ||     D     ||     E     ||     F     ||     G     |
 1|First half of 1986
 2|                   Jan.        Feb.        Mar.        Apr.        May.        Jun.
 3|Income          1100.00      965.00     1245.00     1543.00      875.00      985.00
 4|Expenses         450.00      567.00      982.00      560.00      700.00      854.00
 5|Amount left      650.00      398.00      263.00      983.00      175.00      131.00
 6|
 7|
 8|
 9|
10|
11|
12|
13|
14|
15|
16|
17|
18|
19|
20|
> A1          Text="First half of 1986
£,?,D(ata),G(raph-Type),T(ime-Labs),V(ar-Labs),P(oint-Labs),H(eads) or O(pts)
 7>/View,
```

Figure 7.1a

```
Current graph (#1) -> Bar  Current Device -> EPSON MX100 Printer

HEADINGS:                  SCALING:
Main:     (A1)             Y-Axis: Auto
Sub:      (empty)          X-Axis: Auto
X-Axis:   (empty)
Y-Axis:   (C1)

TIME-LABELS: (B2:G2)

    Data           Pt-Labels      Var-Labels     FORMATS:
A:  (B3:G3)        (empty)        (A3)           Axis:
B:  (B4:G4)        (empty)        (A4)           Time:
C:  (B5:G5)        (empty)        (A5)           Var:
D:  (empty)        (empty)        (empty)        Point:
E:  (empty)        (empty)        (empty)        % :
F:  (empty)        (empty)        (empty)
G:  (empty)        (empty)        (empty)
H:  (empty)        (empty)        (empty)
I:  (empty)        (empty)        (empty)
J:  (empty)        (empty)        (empty)

PIE EXPLOSION: None                 MODE: One variable (A)
```

Figure 7.1b

The L, Layout, option allows you to decide exactly how you want your graphs to be laid out on paper. The screen provided by this last option is shown in Fig. 7.1c.

Before actually committing your graph to paper, you can VIEW it on the screen. On the Apricot this is done by pressing the VIEW key on the microscreen; Control-T has the same effect. If you are satisfied with your graph, you can select PRINT on the microscreen and switch the printer on; Control-Y is the alternative command. The printing of the

```
LAYOUT SELECTIONS FOR PLOTTER

Page Size:             * "Page Size describes the physical paper you are using
Paper          2         with your graphics printer or plotter. Page Width is the
Width      14.00         direction along which the paper is normally read.
Length     11.00       * "Graph Size" describes where, how large and in which
                          direction the graph is drawn.
Graph Size:            * Size, Rotation and Offset adjsut automatically EXCEPT in
Mode           F         Manual Mode. In Manual Mode you can change graph settings.
Rotation       H       * In Horizontal Rotation the graph is viewed in the normal
                         reading direction of the paper. Vertical Rotation is the
Width      13.00         opposite of Horizontal.
Length     10.00       * Graph Width is approximately 1.3 times Graph Length for
                         most graphics devices. If this "aspect ratio" is changed
Graph/Page Offset:       (allowed only in Manual Mode) you Pie graphs will look
Top         0.50         like watermelons. If you set Graph Width OR Length to 0.00
Left        0.50         SuperCalc3 substitutes an appropriate value using the
                         aspect ratio of your device.
                       * "Graph/Page Offset" tells SuperCalc3 where on the page
                         (measured from the Top and Left) to start the graph.

1 = 8.5" X 11";  2 = 14" X 11":
 24>/Global,Graphics,Layout
```

Figure 7.1c

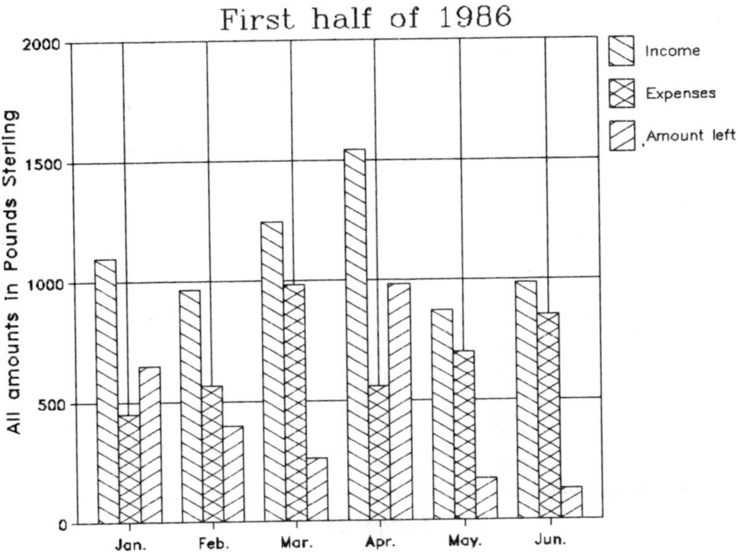

Figure 7.2

graph can be quite a lengthy business. For the graphs shown in this book the average time was about fifteen minutes each. The more expensive and sophisticated the printer or plotter, the faster your graph will be drawn. The completed graph is shown in Fig. 7.2.

Example 1 — The cashflow example — part 3

Now you are in a position to complete the cashflow example by displaying some of the information it contains in graphical form. The first thing you do is to display the production costs in the form of a bar chart, the specifications for which are shown in Fig. 7.3a. The sales and office expenses are shown by means of a straight line graph specified as shown in Fig. 7.3b. The resulting graphs are shown in Figs. 7.4 and 7.5.

```
Current graph (£1) -> Bar  Current Device -> EPSON MX100 Printer

HEADINGS:                  SCALING:
Main:     (E1)             Y-Axis: Auto
Sub:      (A9)             X-Axis: Auto
X-Axis:   (empty)
Y-Axis:   (empty)

TIME-LABELS: (E4:J4)

   Data           Pt-Labels     Var-Labels     FORMATS:
A: (E11:J11)      (empty)       (A11)          Axis:
B: (E10:J10)      (empty)       (A10)          Time:
C: (E12:J12)      (empty)       (A12)          Var:
D: (E13:J13)      (empty)       (A13)          Point:
E: (empty)        (empty)       (empty)        % :
F: (empty)        (empty)       (empty)
G: (empty)        (empty)       (empty)
H: (empty)        (empty)       (empty)
I: (empty)        (empty)       (empty)
J: (empty)        (empty)       (empty)

PIE EXPLOSION: None               MODE: One Variable (A)
```

Figure 7.3a

```
Current graph (#2) -> Line Current Device -> EPSON MX100 Printer

HEADINGS:                  SCALING:
Main:     (E1)             Y-Axis: Auto
Sub:      (A15)            X-Axis: Auto
X-Axis:   (empty)
Y-Axis:   (empty)
TIME-LABELS: (E4:J4)

   Data           Pt-Labels     Var-Labels     FORMATS:
A: (E16:J16)      (empty)       (A16)          Axis:
B: (E17:J17)      (empty)       (A17)          Time:
C: (E18:J18)      (empty)       (A18)          Var:
D: (E19:J19)      (empty)       (A19)          Point:
E: (E20:J20)      (empty)       (A20)          % :
F: (E21:J21)      (empty)       (A21)
G: (empty)        (empty)       (empty)
H: (empty)        (empty)       (empty)
I: (empty)        (empty)       (empty)
J: (empty)        (empty)       (empty)

PIE EXPLOSION: None               MODE: One Variable (A)
```

Figure 7.3b

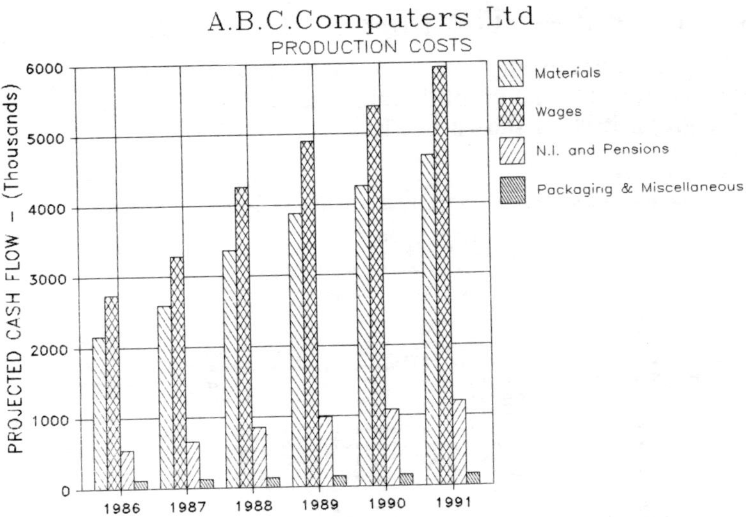

Figure 7.4

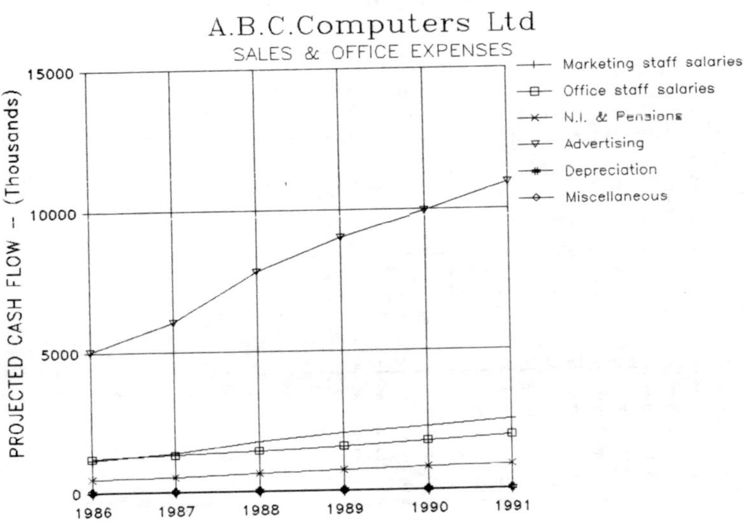

Figure 7.5

Example 2 — The time series — part 3

The time series example can now also be completed, and the specification for the graph parameters is shown in Fig. 7.6a. The graph itself is shown in Fig. 7.7.

```
Current graph (#1) -> Line Current Device -> EPSON MX100 Printer

HEADINGS:                          SCALING:
Main:     (empty)                  Y-Axis: Auto
Sub:      (empty)                  X-Axis: Auto
X-Axis:   (empty)
Y-Axis:   (empty)

TIME-LABELS: (A2:A17)

   Data             Pt-Labels      Var-Labels      FORMATS:
A: (C2:C17)         (empty)        (C1)            Axis:
B: (C29:C33)        (empty)        (A28)           Time:
C: (G2:G21)         (empty)        (G1)            Var:
D: (empty)          (empty)        (empty)         Point:
E: (empty)          (empty)        (empty)         % :
F: (empty)          (empty)        (empty)
G: (empty)          (empty)        (empty)
H: (empty)          (empty)        (empty)
I: (empty)          (empty)        (empty)
J: (empty)          (empty)        (empty)

PIE EXPLOSION: None                  MODE: One Variable (A)
```

Figure 7.6a

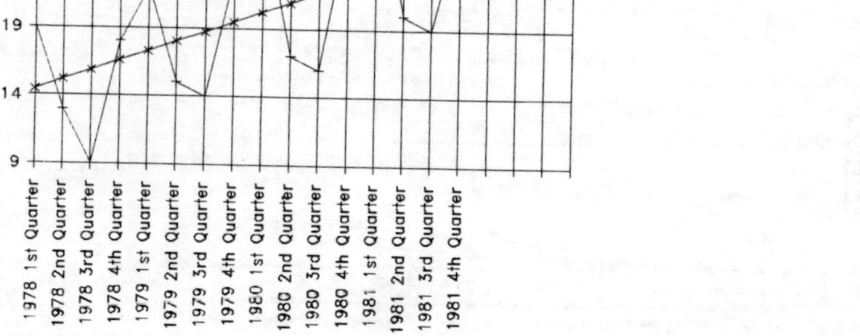

Figure 7.7

Example 3 — The other time series — part 2

For the other time series example, the specification is shown in Fig. 7.8a and the graph itself in Fig. 7.9.

```
Current graph (#1) -> Line Current Device -> EPSON MX100 Printer

HEADINGS:                            SCALING:
Main:      (empty)                   Y-Axis: Auto
Sub:       (empty)                   X-Axis: Auto
X-Axis:    (empty)
Y-Axis:    (A19)

TIME-LABELS: (A21:A26)

    Data             Pt-Labels        Var-Labels        FORMATS:
A: (B21:B26)        (empty)          (B1)              Axis:
B: (C21:C26)        (empty)          (C1)              Time:
C: (D21:D26)        (empty)          (D1)              Var:
D: (E21:E26)        (empty)          (E1)              Point:
E: (empty)          (empty)          (empty)           % :
F: (empty)          (empty)          (empty)
G: (empty)          (empty)          (empty)
H: (empty)          (empty)          (empty)
I: (empty)          (empty)          (empty)
J: (empty)          (empty)          (empty)

PIE EXPLOSION: None                  MODE: One Variable (A)
```

Figure 7.8a

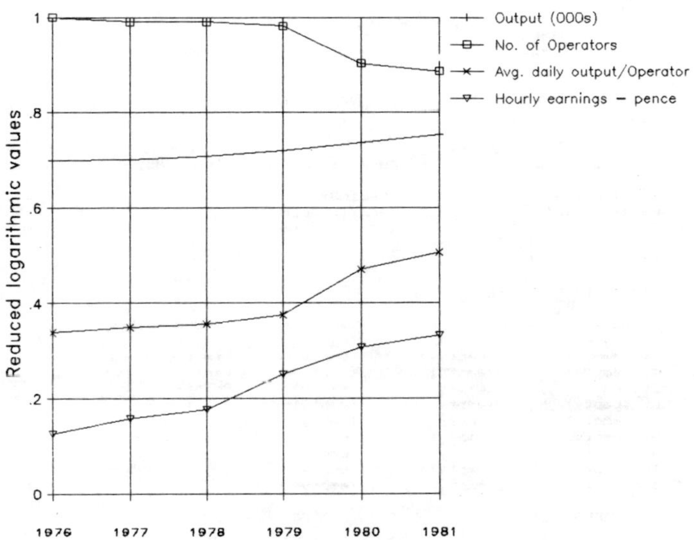

Figure 7.9

Some other graphs

The first spreadsheet you are going to use here is shown in Fig. 7.10. This time you are going to display the information on two pie charts. In the first one, take the O, Options, option from the /V command and from this specify that you want an exploded pie chart with one segment 'exploded'. The specification for the graph is shown in Fig. 7.11a, and you are also going to define some special type faces, or fonts, by using the /GGF command—Global, Graphics, Fonts—and the selection is shown in Fig. 7.11b. Figure 7.12 shows the final pie chart.

The next pie chart from the same sheet chooses to have all the segments exploded and italic type used for the headings and the point labels. This is shown in Fig. 7.13.

The second spreadsheet is a production control chart showing the upper and lower warning limits. The spreadsheet

```
  |    A    ||    B    ||    C    ||    D    ||    E    ||    F    |
 1|A.B.C. Computers Ltd.        Sales of graphics terminals
 2|
 3|          N.AmericaSterling W.Europe Rest of World
 4|      1984       594      1529      1665       622
 5|      1986      1139      1756      2264      1018
```

Figure 7.10

```
Current graph (£1) -> Pie   Current Device -> EPSON MX100 Printer

HEADINGS:                   SCALING:
Main:     (A1)              Y-Axis: Auto
Sub:      (D1)              X-Axis: Auto
X-Axis:   (empty)
Y-Axis:   (empty)

TIME-LABELS: (B3:E3)

    Data            Pt-Labels         Var-Labels        FORMATS:
A:  (B4:E4)         (B4:E4)           (A4)               Axis:
B:  (empty)         (empty)           (empty)           Time:
C:  (empty)         (empty)           (empty)           Var:
D:  (empty)         (empty)           (empty)           Point:
E:  (empty)         (empty)           (empty)             % :
F:  (empty)         (empty)           (empty)
G:  (empty)         (empty)           (empty)
H:  (empty)         (empty)           (empty)
I:  (empty)         (empty)           (empty)
J:  (empty)         (empty)           (empty)

PIE EXPLOSION: 1                      MODE: One Variable (A)
```

Figure 7.11a

```
FONT SELECTION FOR PLOTTER

Headings:                     Labels:
Main           2              Axis        2
Sub            2              Time        2
X-Axis         2              Vars        1
Y-Axis         2              Point       1


1 = Block,  single-stroke
2 = Block,  double-stroke
3 = Roman,  double-stroke
4 = Roman,  triple-stroke
5 = Italic, double-stroke
6 = Italic, triple-stroke
7 = Script, single-stroke
8 = Script, double-stroke



Font number <1-8>:
 23>/Global,Graphics,Fonts
```

Figure 7.11b

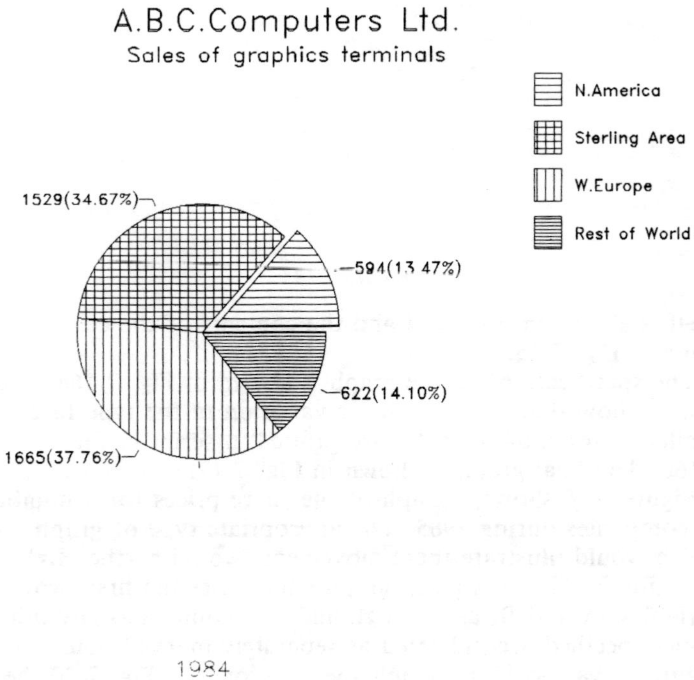

Figure 7.12

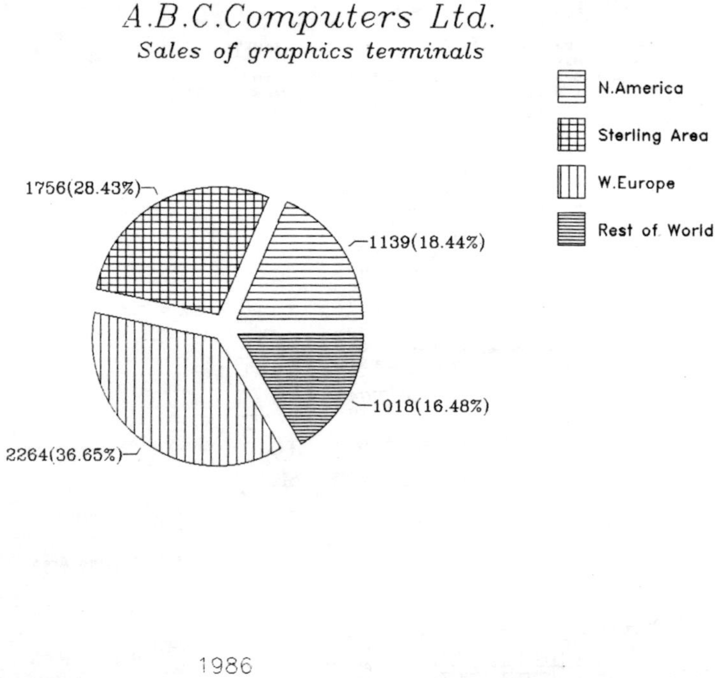

Figure 7.13

itself is shown in Fig. 7.14 and the contents of the cells are listed in Fig. 7.15.

The specification for the graph is shown in Fig. 7.16a, and just to show that there is a wide variation in the type faces available, some of the titles are printed in script in Fig. 7.16b. The final graph is shown in Fig. 7.17.

Figure 7.18 shows a graph of the share prices for a number of companies during 1985. The appropriate type of graph which would illustrate these movements would be the High–Low graph. This is a point graph which uses the first two variables, A and B, as the high and low points and any other values specified are indicated as separately marked points. Figure 7.19a shows the graph specification and Fig. 7.20 the final graph.

	A	B	C	D	E	F	G	H	I	J	K
1		CONTROL CHART									
2		Upper and lower warning limits									
3	Hour	1	2	3	4	5	6	7	8	9	10
4	Production - units	745	750	784	801	711	721	745	789	790	820
5											
6	Sample mean	765.6									
7		424.36	243.36	338.56	1253.16	2981.16	1989.16	424.36	547.56	595.36	2959.36
8	Variance	1175.64									
9	Standard deviation	34.28761									
10	Sigma	36.14231									
11	Upper control limit	847	847	847	847	847	847	847	847	847	847
12	Lower control limit	683	683	683	683	683	683	683	683	683	683

Figure 7.14

```
SuperCalc ver.  1.00

B1      = "CONTROL CHART
B2      = "Upper and lower warning limits
A3      = "Hour
B3      = 1
C3      = 2
D3      = 3
E3      = 4
F3      = 5
G3      = 6
H3      = 7
I3      = 8
J3      = 9
K3      = 10
A4      = "Production - units
B4      = 745
C4      = 750
D4      = 784
E4      = 801
F4      = 711
G4      = 721
H4      = 745
I4      = 789
J4      = 790
K4      = 820
A6      = "Sample mean
B6      = AVERAGE(B4:K4)
B7      = (B4-B6)^2
C7      = (C4-B6)^2
D7      = (D4-B6)^2
E7      = (E4-B6)^2
F7      = (F4-B6)^2
G7      = (G4-B6)^2
H7      = (H4-B6)^2
I7      = (I4-B6)^2
J7      = (J4-B6)^2
K7      = (K4-B6)^2
A8      = "Variance
B8      = AVERAGE(B7:K7)
A9      = "Standard deviation
D7      = SQRT(DO)
A10     = "Sigma
B10     = B9*SQRT(COUNT(B4:K4)/(COUNT(B4:K4)-1))
A11     = "Upper control limit
B11     = INT(B6+B10*2.26)
C11     = B11
D11     = C11
E11     = D11
F11     = E11
G11     = F11
H11     = G11
I11     = H11
J11     = I11
K11     = J11
A12     = "Lower control limit
B12     = INT(B6-2.26*B10)
C12     = B12
D12     = C12
E12     = D12
F12     = E12
G12     = F12
H12     = G12
I12     = H12
J12     = I12
K12     = J12
```

Figure 7.15

```
Current graph (£1) -> X-Y  Current Device -> EPSON MX100 Printer

HEADINGS:                  SCALING:
Main:     (B1)             Y-Axis: Auto
Sub:      (B2)             X-Axis: Auto
X-Axis:   (A3)
Y-Axis:   (A4)

TIME-LABELS: (empty)

   Data          Pt-Labels    Var-Labels    FORMATS:
A: (B3:K6)       (empty)      (empty)       Axis:
B: (B4:K4)       (empty)      (empty)       Time:
C: (B11:K11)     (empty)      (A11)         Var:
D: (B12:K12)     (empty)      (A12)         Point:
E: (empty)       (empty)      (empty)       % :
F: (empty)       (empty)      (empty)
G: (empty)       (empty)      (empty)
H: (empty)       (empty)      (empty)
I: (empty)       (empty)      (empty)
J: (empty)       (empty)      (empty)

PIE EXPLOSION: None             MODE: One Variable (A)
```

Figure 7.16a

```
FONT SELECTION FOR PLOTTER

Headings:                Labels:
Main        7            Axis      2
Sub         7            Time      2
X-Axis      2            Vars      7
Y-Axis      2            Point     7

1 = Block,  single-stroke
2 = Block,  double-stroke
3 = Roman,  double-stroke
4 = Roman,  triple-stroke
5 = Italic, double-stroke
6 = Italic, triple-stroke
7 = Script, single-stroke
8 = Script, double-stroke


Font number <1-8>:
 23>/Global,Graphics,Fonts
```

Figure 7.16b

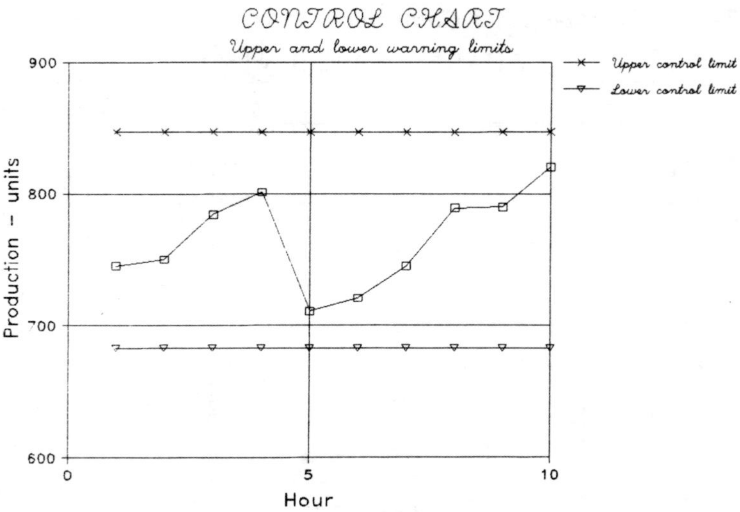

Figure 7.17

	A	B	C	D	E	F
1	SHARE MOVEMENTS		Share value (pence)			
2		Smiths 'A'	Greens Pref	Harris Ord	Jones Holdings	Walters Stores
3	1985 High	450	210	267	231	444
4	1985 Low	230	169	160	122	230
5	Jan 85	255	190	261	140	290
6	Apr 85	290	185	263	220	333
7	Jul 85	389	160	163	230	400
8	Oct 85	440	200	250	160	360

Figure 7.18

```
Current graph (f1) -> Hi-Lo  Current Device -> EPSON MX100 Printer

HEADINGS:                    SCALING:
Main:     (A1)               Y-Axis: Auto
Sub:      (empty)            X-Axis: Auto
X-Axis:   (empty)
Y-Axis:   (C1)

TIME-LABELS: (empty)

   Data          Pt-Labels     Var-Labels     FORMATS:
A: (B3:F3)       (empty)       (A3)           Axis:
B: (B4:F4)       (empty)       (A4)           Time:
C: (B5:F5)       (empty)       (A5)           Var:
D: (B6:F6)       (empty)       (A6)           Point:
E: (B7:F7)       (empty)       (A7)           % :
F: (B8:F8)       (empty)       (A8)
G: (empty)       (empty)       (empty)
H: (empty)       (empty)       (empty)
I: (empty)       (empty)       (empty)
J: (empty)       (empty)       (empty)

PIE EXPLOSION: None                MODE: One Variable (A)
```

Figure 7.19a

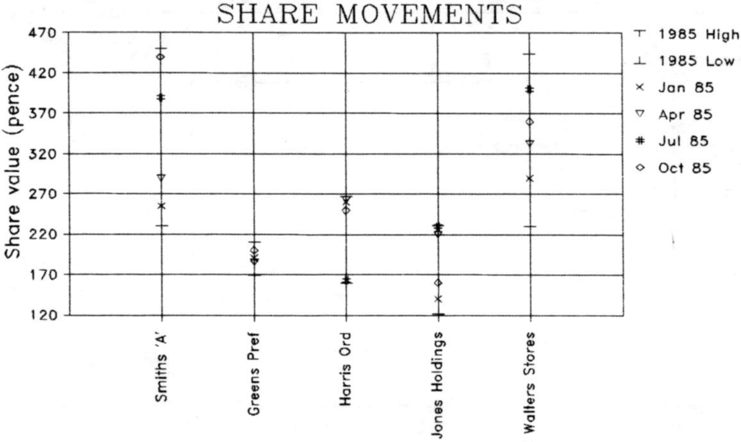

Figure 7.20

Mathematical and statistical graphs are well catered for by SuperCalc3, as the next two examples illustrate. They both use the graph option to plot what SuperCalc3 calls X–Y graphs. The first is the mathematical example where the extreme left-hand and right-hand portions of the sheet are shown in Figs 7.21a and 7.21b. By choosing the X–Y option,

```
  :  A  ::   B   ::   C  ::   D  ::   E  ::   F  ::   G  ::   H  :
 1:
 2:X                     -5    -4.5      -4    -3.5      -3    -2.5
 3:Y      X^2-3*X-5       5    1.75      -1   -3.25      -5   -6.25
 4:       5*X+2         -23   -20.5     -18   -15.5     -13   -10.5
 5:
 6:
 7:
 8:
 9:
10:
11:
12:
13:
14:
15:
16:
17:
18:
19:
20:
< A4
Width:   9   Memory:42 Last Col/Row:AA4        ? for Help
 >1
```

Figure 7.21a

```
  :    T    ::    U    ::    V    ::    W    ::    X    ::    Y    ::    Z    ::   AA   :
 1:
 2:     3.5          4      4.5          5      5.5          6        6.5          7
 3:   17.75         23    28.75         35    41.75         49      56.75         65
 4:    19.5         22     24.5         27     29.5         32       34.5         37
 5:
 6:
 7:
 8:
 9:
10:
11:
12:
13:
14:
15:
16:
17:
18:
19:
20:
< T1
Width:    9    Memory:42 Last Col/Row:AA4          ? for Help
  >1
```

Figure 7.21b

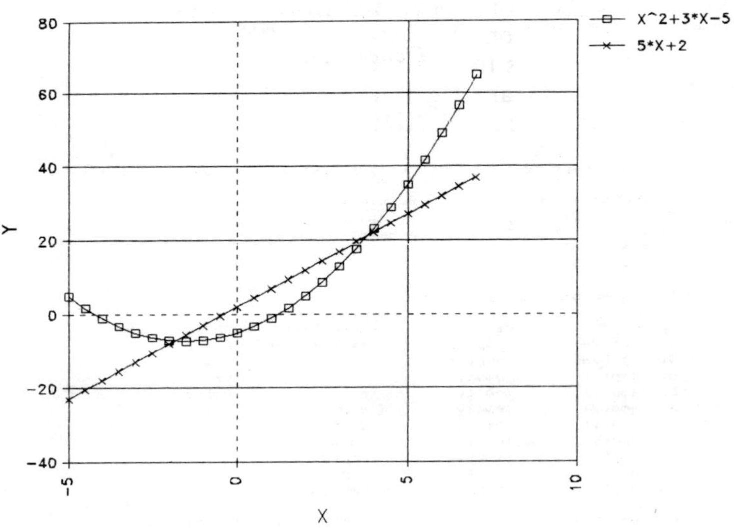

Figure 7.22

the variable defined as variable A is made into the time-base; the horizontal axis and any other variables are plotted relative to that. Figure 7.22 shows the finished graph.

The statistical example is a graph of normal distribution which is plotted from a well-known but complicated formula which uses the standard deviation and mean of a distribution

```
  !   A   !!   B   !!   C   !!   D   !!   E   !!   F   !!   G   !!   H   !
 1!Std. Dev.       .9Graph of normal distribution
 2!Mean          40.8Standard deviation of 0.9; Mean of 40.8
 3!
 4!X        Y
 5!       38 .0000774
 6!    38.25 .0001766
 7!     38.5 .0003733
 8!    38.75 .0007305
 9!       39 .0013233
10!    39.25 .0022191
11!     39.5 .0034450
12!    39.75 .0049509
13!       40 .0065868
14!    40.25 .0081125
15!     40.5 .0092496
16!    40.75 .0097629
17!       41 .0095395
18!    41.25 .0086291
19!     41.5 .0072259
20!    41.75 .0056015
v B5          Form=EXP(-((A5-B2)^2)/(2*B1^2))/SQRT(2*PI*B2^2)
Width:  9  Memory 184  Last Col/Row:C29   ? for HELP
```

Figure 7.23a

```
Current graph (#1) -> X-Y  Current Device -> EPSON MX100 Printer

HEADINGS:                  SCALING:
Main:     (C1)             Y-Axis: Auto
Sub:      (C2)             X-Axis: Auto
X-Axis:   (A4)
Y-Axis:   (B4)

TIME-LABELS: (empty)

   Data            Pt-Labels       Var-Labels      FORMATS:
A: (A5:A29)        (empty)         (empty)         Axis:
B: (B5:B28)        (empty)         (empty)         Time:
C: (empty)         (empty)         (empty)         Var:
D: (empty)         (empty)         (empty)         Point:
E: (empty)         (empty)         (empty)         % :
F: (empty)         (empty)         (empty)
G: (empty)         (empty)         (empty)
H: (empty)         (empty)         (empty)
I: (empty)         (empty)         (empty)
J: (empty)         (empty)         (empty)

PIE EXPLOSION: None                    MODE: One Variable (A)
```

Figure 7.23b

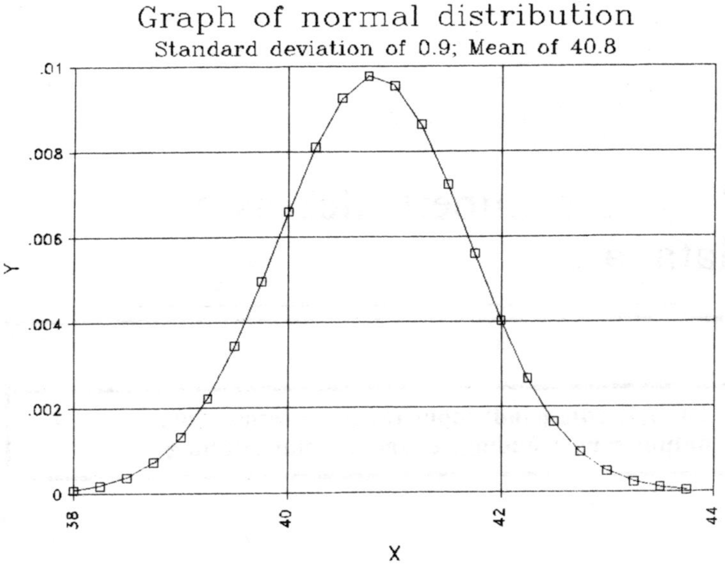

Figure 7.24

to plot a normal curve. The standard formula

$$y = \frac{e^{-(x-\mu)^2/2\sigma^2}}{\sqrt{2\pi\mu^2}}$$

where σ is the standard deviation and μ is the mean, used in this calculation is very complicated to evaluate when only logarithm tables, and even pocket calculators, are used. The facilities offered by a spreadsheet simplify the task dramatically.

Figure 7.23a shows the first part of the sheet where you will notice the formula which is displayed in cell B5. Figure 7.23b shows the specification of the graph which is to be drawn and Fig. 7.24 shows the graph itself.

8 Using SuperCalc3 as a database

The //D command; input range; criterion range; output range; finding, extracting and selecting

The //D command

You can use the information stored in a SuperCalc3 spreadsheet as a database, with each row on the sheet acting as a separate database record. The example shown in Fig. 8.1 shows a list of a number of IBM* PC compatible microcomputers, their prices and other useful information. This data was typed onto a blank spreadsheet from information published in a magazine. It was then sorted into alphabetical order using the /A command.

What you are going to do is to extract a list of computers which satisfy a number of criteria. In order to do this, issue the //D command. Notice that there are two slashes, otherwise you might find that you are accidentally deleting part of your spreadsheet before you know where you are. The display will then look as shown in Fig. 8.2a. The first three options allow you to define where the data being examined is located, the place on the sheet where the

* IBM is a trademark of International Business Machines Corp.

1	TYPE	PRICE	PROCESSOR	Min RAM K	Max RAM K	IBM Keyboard
2	Commodore PC	1675	8088	256	640	N
3	Commodore PC	3000	8088	256	640	N
4	Compaq	2595	8086	256	640	Y
5	Compaq	4080	8086	256	640	Y
6	Compaq Deskpro 286	3990	80286	256	2200	Y
7	Data General/One	2241	80C88	128	512	N
8	Encore	2295	80C86	256	512	N
9	Ericsson	1934	8088	128	640	Y
10	Ericsson	3680	8088	128	640	Y
11	Ericsson Portable	2850	8088	256	512	N
12	Ferranti 860	1350	8086	256	640	N
13	Ferranti 860 XT	2150	8086	256	640	N
14	Gridcase	2975	80C86	128	512	N
15	HP Vectra	3195	80286	512	16000	Y
16	IBM PC	1988	8088	64	640	Y
17	IBM PC AT	3318	80286	256	3000	Y
18	IBM XT	4059	8088	64	640	Y
19	ITT Xtra XP	3595	80286	512	640	N
20	Kaypro 2000	1711	80C88	256	768	N
21	Kaypro 286i	2916	80286	512	640	Y
22	Morrow Pivot	2295	80C88	256	640	N
23	N.Telecom Vienna	3577	80286	640	7000	Y
24	NCR PC8	3448	80286	256	4000	N
25	Paperlogic 80286	4695	80286	512	1000	Y
26	Sharp PC 7000	1795	8086	320	704	N
27	Tandon PCA30	2495	80286	512	16000	Y
28	Televideo AT	2995	80286	256	8000	Y
29	TI Business Pro	3995	80286	512	15000	Y
30	Toshiba	1670	80C88	256	512	N
31	Victor V286	2199	80286	512	15000	Y
32	Visual Commuter	2300	8088	256	512	Y
33	Zenith Z171	2295	80C88	256	640	N
34	Zenith Z200	3295	80286	512	640	Y

Figure 8.1

```
  :          A          ::       B     ::        C      ::      D      :
 1:                  TYPE         PRICE        PROCESSOR       Min RAM K
 2:          Commodore PC          1675             8088             256
 3:          Commodore PC          3000             8088             256
 4:                Compaq          2595             8086             256
 5:                Compaq          4080             8086             256
 6:    Compaq Deskpro 286          3990            80286             256
 7:      Data General/One          2241            80C88             128
 8:                Encore          2295            80C86             256
 9:              Ericsson          1934             8088             128
10:              Ericsson          3680             8088             128
11:     Ericsson Portable          2850             8088             256
12:          Ferranti 860          1350             8086             256
13:       Ferranti 860 XT          2150             8086             256
14:              Gridcase          2975            80C86             128
15:             HP Vectra          3195            80286             512
16:                IBM PC          1988             8088              64
17:             IBM PC AT          3318            80286             256
18:                IBM XT          4059             8088              64
19:          ITT Xtra XP           3595            80286             512
20:          Kaypro 2000           1711            80C88             256
< A1           Text="TYPE
I(nput), C(riterion), O(utput), F(ind), E(xtract), S(elect), R(emain)?
  8>//Data,
```

Figure 8.2a

expressions which allow you to 'sieve' that information have been placed, and the position on the sheet where any list of the selected machines will be displayed.

Input range

If you choose the I (Input range) option you will find that the Prompt Line and the Entry Line beneath it will read

Input range (now empty), ⟨–⟩ to clear
14⟩//Data,Input,

and for this example you will specify that your data block will range from cell A1 in the top left-hand corner down to F100 at the bottom right-hand corner. This is done in order to accommodate additions to your list at some future date. So the two lines now look like this:

Input range (now empty), ⟨–⟩ to clear
21⟩//Data,Input,A1:F100

You should notice that this block includes the titles, which must be there, as well as the data itself. These titles serve to identify the columns of data.

Criterion range

The next thing to do is to choose not only what criteria you are going to apply to the data but where you are going to place it on the sheet. For this example you are going to select all those machines that cost more than £2000, but less than £3000, have a minimum RAM of more than 256K bytes and an IBM compatible keyboard. This time, select the C (Criterion range) option

```
Criterion range (now empty), <-> to clear
18>//Data,Criterion,
```

and you are going to write them in the block H1:J2. This block must include the names of the columns being tested together with the tests to be made on the data contained in those columns. The criteria block has the expression

```
AND(B2>2000,B2<3000)
```

in cell H2,

```
D2>256
```

in cell I2 and **Y** in cell J2. You should notice that the cells referred to in the criterion tests refer to the first cell in the column where the data to be tested is found. As a progression is made down each column SuperCalc3, as usual, adjusts the reference of the active cell.

Output range

All that remains for you to do is to define the block of cells where the selected data is to be displayed. This will be shown as

```
Output range (now empty), <-> to clear
23>//Data,Output,K6:L100
```

with the headings of the required table placed in cells K6 and L6. Again, the headings are important as this tells SuperCalc3 what columns are to be transferred to this part of the sheet.

	A	B	C	D	E	F	G	H	I	J	K	L
1	TYPE	PRICE	PROCESSOR	Min RAM K	Max RAM K	IBM Keyboard		PRICE	MAX RAM	IBM Keyboard		
2	Commodore PC	1675	8088	256	640	N		AND(B2>2000,B2<3000)	B2>256	Y		
3	Commodore PC	3000	8088	256	640	N						
4	Compaq	2595	8086	256	640	Y						
5	Compaq	4080	8086	256	640	Y						
6	Compaq Deskpro 286	3990	80286	256	2200	Y					TYPE	PRICE
7	Data General/One	2241	80C88	128	512	N					Compaq	2595
8	Encore	2295	80C86	256	512	N					Kaypro 286i	2916
9	Ericsson	1934	8088	128	640	Y					Televideo AT	2995
10	Ericsson	3680	8088	128	640	Y					Victor V286	2199
11	Ericsson Portable	2850	8088	256	512	N					Visual Commuter	2300
12	Ferranti 860	1350	8086	256	640	N						
13	Ferranti 860 IT	2150	8086	256	640	N						
14	Gridcase	2975	80C86	128	512	N						
15	HP Vectra	3195	80286	512	16000	Y						
16	IBM PC	1988	8088	64	640	Y						
17	IBM PC AT	3318	80286	256	3000	Y						
18	IBM XT	4059	8088	64	640	Y						
19	ITT Xtra XP	3595	80286	512	640	N						
20	Kaypro 2000	1711	80C88	256	768	N						
21	Kaypro 286i	2916	80286	512	640	Y						
22	Morrow Pivot	2295	80C88	256	640	N						
23	N.Telecom Vienna	3577	80286	640	7000	Y						
24	NCR PC8	3448	80286	256	4000	N						
25	Paperlogic 80286	4695	80286	512	1000	Y						
26	Sharp PC 7000	1795	8086	320	704	N						
27	Tandon PCA30	2495	80286	512	16000	Y						
28	Televideo AT	2995	80286	256	8000	Y						
29	TI Business Pro	3995	80286	512	15000	Y						
30	Toshiba	1670	80C88	256	512	N						
31	Victor V286	2199	80286	512	15000	Y						
32	Visual Commuter	2300	8088	256	512	Y						
33	Zenith Z171	2295	80C88	256	640	N						
34	Zenith Z200	3295	80286	512	640	Y						

Figure 8.3

	A	B	C	D	E	F	G	H	I	J	K	L
1	TYPE	PRICE	PROCESSOR	Min RAM K	Max RAM K	IBM Keyboard		PRICE	MAX RAM	IBM Keyboard		
2	Commodore PC	1675	8088	256	640	N		AND(B2>2000,B2<3000)	D2>256	Y		
3	Commodore PC	3000	8088	256	640	N		B2<=2000	D2>=256			
4	Compaq	2595	8086	256	640	Y						
5	Compaq	4080	8086	256	640	Y						
6	Compaq Deskpro 286	3990	80286	256	2200	Y					TYPE	PRICE
7	Data General/One	2241	80C88	128	512	N					Commodore PC	1675
8	Encore	2295	80C86	256	512	N					Compaq	2595
9	Ericsson	1934	8088	128	640	Y					Ericsson	1934
10	Ericsson	3680	8088	128	640	Y					Ferranti 860	1350
11	Ericsson Portable	2850	8088	256	512	N					IBM PC	1988
12	Ferranti 860	1350	8086	256	640	N					Kaypro 2000	1711
13	Ferranti 860 XT	2150	8086	256	640	N					Kaypro 286i	2916
14	Gridcase	2975	80C86	128	512	N					Sharp PC 7000	1795
15	HP Vectra	3195	80286	512	16000	Y					Televideo AT	2995
16	IBM PC	1988	8088	64	640	Y					Toshiba	1670
17	IBM PC AT	3318	80286	256	3000	Y					Victor V286	2199
18	IBM XT	4059	8088	64	640	Y					Visual Commuter	2300
19	ITT Xtra XP	3595	80286	512	640	N						
20	Kaypro 2000	1711	80C88	256	768	N						
21	Kaypro 286i	2916	80286	512	640	Y						
22	Morrow Pivot	2295	80C88	256	640	N						
23	N.Telecom Vienna	3577	80286	640	7000	Y						
24	NCR PC8	3448	80286	256	4000	N						
25	Paperlogic 80286	4695	80286	512	1000	Y						
26	Sharp PC 7000	1795	8086	320	704	N						
27	Tandon PCA30	2495	80286	512	16000	Y						
28	Televideo AT	2995	80286	256	8000	Y						
29	TI Business Pro	3995	80286	512	15000	Y						
30	Toshiba	1670	80C88	256	512	N						
31	Victor V286	2199	80286	512	15000	Y						
32	Visual Commuter	2300	8088	256	512	Y						
33	Zenith Z171	2295	80C88	256	640	N						
34	Zenith Z200	3295	80286	512	640	Y						

Figure 8.4

Finding, extracting and selecting

Once you have set up the selection criteria, then the process of extracting the relevant data can be carried out. If you select the F (Find) option, then the criteria will be set into operation and the main data table is scanned and the records which fulfil the criteria are highlighted one after the other. Pressing the ↓ and ↑ keys will allow you to move down or up through the selected records. The ← and → keys will allow you to move horizontally through any selected record to view fields not displayed on the screen.

If you choose the E (Extract) option the selected records, or those parts specified by the headings you have put in, will be displayed in the output block. This is shown in Fig. 8.3. You should note that here the contents of the criterion block are displayed as the /GF command was selected before the sheet was printed out.

The S (Select) option works as the previous two options combined. Each Selected record is highlighted and you are given the option of transferring it to the output block.

Selection can be made on more than one set of criteria as is shown in Fig. 8.4. In this case the output block is defined as H1:J3 and a further set of tests are specified in the partial row H3:J3. What then happens is that the selection is made of every record which fulfils the tests given in the first row or the second row. You should note that if one of the specified criterion fields is left empty, as J3 is, then the entry in that column can have any value.

9 e(X)ecute (.XQT) files

Setting up an .XQT file; another example

Setting up an .XQT file

A SuperCalc3 .XQT (called a 'dot' XQT file) file provides you with a means of storing a set of SuperCalc3 commands so that by running the file you are saved the need for continually keying a sometimes complex series of command letters. This is of particular value when you have to perform the samc repetitive operation over and over again. An .XQT file can be set up either from within SuperCalc3 itself or by means of a wordprocessing program such as WordStar. The first example is another version of a process carried out in an earlier chapter. Three separate files are consolidated into one single file and this requires a series of very similar instructions to be issued to SuperCalc3. The blank form is loaded first, then the first monthly information, followed by the second and finally the third. Then you would need to print the complete spreadsheet. An .XQT file contains the actual keystrokes you would make and would look like this:

```
/ZY
/LTOTEX,A
/LJANEX,PA3:G4,A3
/LFEBEX,PA3:G4,A5
```

```
/LMAREX,PA3:G4,A7
/GB
/ODALL,P
/ZY
```

The first line is the command to 'ZAP' the current spreadsheet into order to clear out any cells which may be occupied. The 'Y' is the answer to the question that the /Z command issues, "Yes, we do want to Zap everything". The next command is to load, /L, the file called TOTEX, and All of it. Then load the file called JANEX, but only Part of it, the part specified by the range A3:G4. You want to load it into the part of the current sheet starting at cell A3. The same thing is done to load the block of cells from A3 to G4 of the next two sheets, FEBEX and MAREX. They are loaded at cells A5 and A7 respectively. The /GB command is the Global command to switch off the borders and the next command is to output, /O, the sheet with ALL its contents onto the Printer. Finally, Zap the sheet clear ready for your next job.

If you are entering the commands through SuperCalc3, then you must enter them as text by prefixing each line with a " symbol. You must also switch off the borders so that your sheet looks just as shown above. To save your file, you Output it to a disk file; you must ensure that you name it and add an .XQT extension, otherwise SuperCalc3 will automatically place a .PRN extension after the name.

A .XQT file entered through, say, WordStar, is just entered as a text file so that it looks exactly as shown previously.

To use a .XQT file you will have to select the /X command and enter the filename, with no need of the extension. Then sit back and watch! You will see the commands flick up at the bottom of the screen and the answers to all the questions will be entered automatically.

Another example

A company sells training films, some of which are American in origin. When a copy of a certain film, which can be in

```
  :          A            ::  B  ::     C    ::       D       ::        E       ::  F  ::  G  ::  H  ::  I  :
 1:Dollar rate of exchange  1.51
 2:Processing cost/metre
 3:Colour:                  2.50
 4:Black/white              .55
 5:
 6:TITLE                            Length - m  USA royalty - $ UK price - £
 7:=================================================================================================================
 8:Sailing                 ("Col.") 750        80                IF(B8="Col.",C8*B3+D8/B1,C8*B4+D8/B1)
 9:Saint Anthony           ("Col.") 650        75                IF(B9="Col.",C9*B3+D9/B1,C9*B4+D9/B1)
10:Salesmanship Pt.1       ("B/W")  400        50                IF(B10="Col.",C10*B3+D10/B1,C10*B4+D10/B1)
11:Salesmanship Pt.2       ("B/W")  550        55                IF(B11="Col.",C11*B3+D11/B1,C11*B4+D11/B1)
12:San Francisco           ("B/W")  720        85                IF(B12="Col.",C12*B3+D12/B1,C12*B4+D12/B1)
13:San Remo                ("Col.") 250        60                IF(B13="Col.",C13*B3+D13/B1,C13*B4+D13/B1)
14:Souffle making          ("Col.") 200        55                IF(B14="Col.",C14*B3+D14/B1,C14*B4+D14/B1)
15:Supper dishes           ("Col.") 345        65                IF(B15="Col.",C15*B3+D15/B1,C15*B4+D15/B1)
16:Surfboarding            ("Col.") 300        55                IF(B16="Col.",C16*B3+D16/B1,C16*B4+D16/B1)
17:Sydney Harbour          ("Col.") 235        40                IF(B17="Col.",C17*B3+D17/B1,C17*B4+D17/B1)
```

Figure 9.1

colour or black and white, is sold a royalty is paid to the producer in the USA and the selling price is made up of that cost plus the cost of producing the copy. There are three variables which have to be taken into account whenever a new price list is made up. These are the rate of exchange, dollars per pound sterling, the cost per metre of copying colour film and the cost per metre of processing black and white film. The spreadsheet for the price list with its embedded formulae is shown in Fig. 9.1.

In order to make the task of creating a new price list as simple as possible, the following .XQT file can be used:

```
/ZY
/GM
/LFILMS,A
=B1
&
=B3
&
=B4
&
!
/GB
/ODALL,P
/QY
```

```
   :  A  ::  B  ::  C  ::  D  ::  E  ::  F  ::  G  ::  H  :
  1:
  2:
  3:
  4:
  5:
  6:
  7:
  8:
  9:
 10:
 11:
 12:
 13:
 14:
 15:
 16:
 17:
 18:
 19:
 20:
> A1
Enter File Name (or <RETURN> for directory)
 18>/X(Execute),rates
```

Figure 9.1a

Dollar rate of exchange	1.49
Processing cost/metre	
Colour:	2.6
Black/white	.56

TITLE		Length - m	USA royalty - $	UK price - £
Sailing	Col.	750	80.00	2003.69
Saint Anthony	Col.	650	75.00	1740.34
Salesmanship Pt.1	B/W	400	50.00	257.56
Salesmanship Pt.2	B/W	550	55.00	344.91
San Francisco	B/W	720	85.00	460.25
San Remo	Col.	250	60.00	690.27
Souffle making	Col.	200	55.00	556.91
Supper dishes	Col.	345	65.00	940.62
Surfboarding	Col.	300	55.00	816.91
Sydney Harbour	Col.	235	40.00	637.85

Figure 9.2

The ' = ' sign is the SuperCalc3 'GoTo' instruction, followed by the cell reference, and the '&' sign is the instruction to drop out of the .XQT file and await for input from the keyboard. Each keyboard input has to be terminated by a Return followed by another '&' to return you to the .XQT file.

These three inputs allow you to change the dollar rate of exchange and the two processing costs. Because the Manual option for recalculation was chosen from the Global command, /GM, the sheet is recalculated when the '!' is entered. The borders are then removed, the sheet printed and the /QY takes you out of SuperCalc3. The state of the screen just prior to using the .XQT file, called RATES.XQT, is shown in Fig. 9.1a. The final result is shown in Fig. 9.2.

10 Interfacing with other programs

Reading a dBASE II file into a spreadsheet and processing it with a .XQT file; converting a spreadsheet into dBASE format

Reading a dBASE II file into a spreadsheet and processing it with a .XQT file

If you have a database file that was created by the dBASE II* or dBASE III* programs, then it can be read into a SuperCalc3 spreadsheet by using one facility of dBASE and one facility of SuperCalc3. The dBASE file used for this example has the structure shown in Fig. 10.1 and the contents of the file are shown in Fig. 10.2. First of all the records on the database file have to be converted into a form in which they are delimited, separated, by commas. As SuperCalc3 recognizes the difference between text and numbers by the characters an entry contains, then the resulting file is ready for conversion into SuperCalc3 format. This file is created by the dBASE command

```
COPY TO SALES DELIMITED WITH ,
```

*dBASE II and dBASE III are trademarks of Ashton-Tate.

and the resulting file will be known, automatically, as SALES.TXT. You then leave dBASE.

Then the SDI program (Super Data Interchange) is used, and you use option B, as shown in Fig. 10.3, to convert the file separated by commas into a .CAL file. Now SuperCalc3 is run and the following .XQT file will produce the result

```
Structure for file: A:SALES    .DBF
Number of records: 00015
Date of last update: 05/07/86
Primary use database
Fld     Name     Type    Width    Dec
001       SURNAME       C      020
002       INITIALS      C      006
003       TARGET        N      008      002
004       AREA          C      006
** Total **                  00041
```

Figure 10.1

```
00001  Green              S.L.     10000.00 002
00002  Harris             T.L.     50000.00 006
00003  Johnson            R.       45000.00 010
00004  Kemworthy          P.J.H.   35000.00 011
00005  Donn               P.J.     65000.00 004
00006  Blake              R.T.     25000.00 008
00007  Long               A.       75000.00 015
00008  Grange             G.J.     35000.00 007
00009  Norris             C.J.     27500.00 005
00010  Ladnier            T.       85000.00 021
00011  Francis            T.K.     15000.00 002
00012  Harris             P.K.     12500.00 005
00013  Bangor             I.       18000.00 007
00014  Kelly              S.M.     17500.00 001
00015  Jacobs             L.J.     10000.00 008
```

Figure 10.2

```
                  Sorcim File Conversion Utility
                          Version : 1.12
                  ------------------------------
                These are the File Conversions Available :
A. SuperCalc file to Comma Separated Value file
B. Comma Separated Value file to SuperCalc file
C. SuperCalc file to SuperData Format file
D. SuperData Format file to SuperClac file
X. Exit program

             Enter Your choice (A, B, C, D, or X) ? B

Enter Source File Name : sales.txt
Opening file : sales.txt

Enter Destination File Name : sales
```

Figure 10.3

Name	Initials	Target - £	Area
Bangor	I.	18000	7
Blake	R.T.	25000	8
Donn	P.J.	65000	4
Francis	T.K.	15000	2
Grange	G.J.	35000	7
Green	S.L.	10000	2
Harris	T.L.	50000	6
Harris	P.K.	12500	5
Jacobs	L.J.	10000	8
Johnson	R.	45000	10
Kelly	S.M.	17500	1
Kemworthy	P.J.H.	35000	11
Ladnier	T.	85000	21
Long	A.	75000	15
Norris	C.J.	27500	5

Figure 10.4

shown in Fig. 10.4 on the printer.

```
/ZY
/LSALES,A
/ACA
/IR1
=A1
"Name
=B1
"Initials
=C1
"Target — £
=D1
"Area
=A1
/FCC,12,L
/FCD,L
/GB
/ODALL,P
```

Converting a spreadsheet into dBASE format

The reverse process of converting a SuperCalc3 file into dBASE format is performed by the SDI program, only this time using the A option. For this example, use the spreadsheet shown in Fig. 8.3. The criterion and output

```
                    Sorcim File Conversion Utility
                            Version : 1.12

                    --------------------------------
                  These are the File Conversions Available :
A. SuperCalc file to Comma Separated Value file
B. Comma Separated Value file to SuperCalc file
C. SuperCalc file to SuperData Format file
D. SuperData Format file to SuperClac file
X. Exit program

              Enter Your choice (A, B, C, D, or X) ? B

Enter Source File Name : micro1
Opening file : micro1.CAL

Enter Destination File Name : micro1
Opening file : micro1.CSV

Converting  micro1.CAL to micro1.CSV
```

Figure 10.5

blocks have been deleted and the remainder, which consists of the list of microcomputers and their features, are saved in SuperCalc3 format on a file called MICRO1.CAL by using the /S, Save, command. The first part of the conversion takes place using SDI as shown in Fig. 10.5. You now have a 'comma separated value' or .CSV file.

The next move is to go into the dBASE II program and create a file which is going to receive the data. In this case it is an empty file called MICRO.DBF. As you are going to APPEND the data onto the file, it could be empty or contain some records already. The sequence is shown in Fig. 10.6 and ends up with the contents of the new database file listed out.

```
 . list structure
Structure for file: A:MICRO   .DBF
Number of records: 00000
Date of last update: 05/07/86
Primary use database
Fld    Name    Type    Width   Dec
001      TYPE          C      020
002      PRICE         N      004
003      PROCESSOR     C      005
004      MINRAM        N      003
005      MAXRAM        N      005
006      IBMKEY        C      001
** Total **                 00039
 . list
 . append from micro1.csv delimited
00033 records added
 . list
00001   Commodore PC            1675 8088    256     640 N
00002   Commodore PC            3000 8088    256     640 N
00003   Compaq                  2595 8086    256     640 Y
00004   Compaq                  4080 8086    256     640 Y
00005   Compaq Deskpro 286      3990 80286   256    2200 Y
00006   Data General/One        2241 80C88   128     512 N
00007   Encore                  2295 80C86   256     512 N
00008   Ericsson                1934 8088    128     640 Y
00009   Ericsson                3680 8088    128     640 Y
00010   Ericsson Portable       2850 8088    256     512 N
00011   Ferranti 860            1350 8086    256     640 N
00012   Ferranti 860 XT         2150 8086    256     640 N
00013   Gridcase                2975 80C86   128     512 N
00014   HP Vectra               3195 80286   512   16000 Y
00015   IBM PC                  1988 8088     64     640 Y
00016   IBM PC AT               3318 80286   256    3000 Y
00017   IBM XT                  4059 8088     64     640 Y
00018   ITT Xtra XP             3595 80286   512     640 N
00019   Kaypro 2000             1711 80C88   256     768 N
00020   Kaypro 286i             2916 80286   512     640 Y
00021   Morrow Pivot            2295 80C88   256     640 N
00022   N.Telecom Vienna        3577 80286   640    7000 Y
00023   NCR PC8                 3448 80286   256    4000 N
00024   Paperlogic 80286        4695 80286   512    1000 Y
00025   Sharp PC 7000           1795 8086    320     704 N
00026   Tandon PCA30            2495 80286   512   16000 T
00027   Televideo AT            2995 80286   256    8000 Y
00028   TI Business Pro         3995 80286   512   15000 Y
00029   Toshiba                 1670 80C88   256     512 N
00030   Victor V286             2199 80286   512   15000 Y
00031   Visual Commuter         2300 8088    256     512 Y
00032   Zenith Z171             2295 80C88   256     640 N
00033   Zenith Z200             3295 80286   512     640 Y
```

Figure 10.6

11 SuperCalc3, Release 2.1

Features of Release 2.1; iteration; the RAN function; the SIDEWAYS program

Features of Release 2.1

The latest version of SuperCalc3, issued after this Companion was commenced, provides a number of very powerful new features. The first of these is that the size of the spreadsheet has been increased considerably. In fact, 127 columns and 9999 rows are available, providing your computer has sufficient memory. The extreme right-hand lower corner of your spreadsheet can now be cell DW9999. The database option has been enhanced so that almost ten thousand records with up to 127 fields per record can be accommodated. If your computer is fitted with the 8087 arithmetic unit, then the speed of calculation is increased ten-fold.

You can now choose from the /G (Global) command whether all text need be prefixed by the " symbol or not. The new list of options from this command are given as

Optimum,Keep,Graphics,Form,",Next,Border,Tab,Prot,Row /Col/Dep,IterS,Man/Auto

The Optimum option makes it possible for you to allocate memory space in such a way as to have a lot of space for

```
OPTIMUM SPREADSHEET CONDITIONS MENU [F2 to return to spreadsheet]
To change and "Current setting" for FUTURE work sessions (not this session):
(1) Save spreadsheet. (2) Select new setting. (3) Enter /Global,Keep, then /Quit.

MEMORY:  Select F for faster performance, but less spreadsheet data-space in
memory, or D for maximum spreadsheet data Data-space, but slower performance.
  Current setting:     F      Setting will be:   D

SPREADSHEET BOUNDARY: Increasing boundary decreases memory available for data.
Small    -  63 columns x  254 rows max. Provides most data-space in memory.
Medium - 127 columns x 2000 rows max. Provides 4k less data-space than Small.
Large   - 127 columns x 9999 rows max. Provides 20k less data-space than Small.
Automatic - SuperCalc3 picks boundaries (S or M) based on available memory.
  Current setting:     A      Setting willbe:       L

SCREEN:  I for IBM-PC & most compatibles, C for Compaq, or H for Hercules.
  Current setting:      I      Setting will be:    I



I(BM & most compatibles), C(ompaq), or H(ercules)
 17>/Global,Optimum
F1=Help F2=Cancel F9=Plot  F10=View
```

Figure 11.1a

data but slower execution, or faster execution with a smaller amount of memory space.

The full-screen menu produced by this option is shown in Fig. 11.1a.

The Keep option allows you to retain settings obtained from the full-screen menus; graphics defaults, printer defaults, data disk drive defaults and the Optimum settings. These then become immediately available on loading SuperCalc3.

The Graphics and Form options are as before.

The " option is the one to force all text to be preceded with the " character. It is an on/off toggle. Next, which causes an automatic advance of the cursor position when Return is pressed, and Border are also toggles. Tab, when set on, causes the cursor to jump to the next unprotected cell which contains a blank.

The Prot (Protect) toggle will remove all protection from cells which have been protected by the /P, Protect, command, when it is on. The protection can be reimposed and all the protected cells are safe again.

The Row/Col/Dep options refer to the order in which calculation takes place. The first forces calculation to take place across the columns row by row, the second forces calculation to take place column by column down the rows.

The third option is a natural dependency option so that the calculation defined in any cell does not take place until all the references in that cell are calculated. If there are so-called circular references, as in iterative calculations, then the CIRC prompt appears at the top left-hand corner of the screen.

IterS is the iteration control option which is dealt with in the next section.

The Man/Auto option is the same as in previous versions of SuperCalc3 so that you can choose to have recalculation only on pressing the ! (Recalc) key, or automatic recalculation each time a new entry is made on the sheet.

From the /F (Format) command you now have the choice of having text centred as well as left or right justified. Cell ranges can now be specified by using a period, full stop, as well as a colon. This means that the range

A12:CA999

can be written also as

A12.CA999

Iteration

A powerful new feature of Release 2.1 is its ability to perform iterative calculations. In this type of problem a series of numbers incremented by a fixed amount are fed into one or more formulae in sequence. It is a technique used in mathematics to produce an accurate solution to an equation from an initial 'guess' which is continually refined to become closer and closer to the correct solution.

A simple example of this is the calculation of a square root. It is in fact the method used by calculators and computers to evaluate square roots. The routine is to go through the following process

Take your first guess at the square root to be 1. Then calculate the arithmetic mean of the guess and the number divided by the guess. If the result of this calculation is not equal to the guess, use the answer you obtained as the next guess. Perform this operation until the guess you put into the calculation and the answer you get from it are the same or you have performed the iteration more than 20 times. The resulting number is the square root of the original number.

The first thing to do is use the /G, Global, command, so that Manual recalculation is set. The contents of the sheet are shown in Fig. 11.2. The ITER variable kept by SuperCalc3 is a count of the number of times the iteration is performed. The contents of cell B6 says that if the iteration count, held in ITER, is equal to 1, then place 1 in the cell, otherwise place the contents of B8 in the cell. B8 contains the result of the calculation

(B6 + B3/B6)/2

The entries in B1 and B8 are hidden by taking the H option from the Format line. The entry in B1 is the device used to stop the iteration when ITER reaches the value of 21. This is used in conjunction with the /GI (Global command, Iteration control option) command. If you then choose the Solve option from this you can specify that the iteration control cell is, in this case, cell B1.

The first number is the increment test to be used after ITER reaches 21; a very large value which would deal with any divergence which might be happening. Up to that point the iteration is allowed to continue providing the difference between successive calculated values exceeds 0.001. If the difference between these values is less than 0.001 before ITER reaches 21, the iteration stops automatically. The display is shown in Fig. 11.3 after the calculation has taken place.

You can, if you wish, omit the control cell B1 and opt to use a predefined number of iterations. This is obtained from

```
SuperCalc, ver.  2.1

B1 H      = IF(ITER>=21,10000,.001)
A3        = "Square root of:
B3        = 99.99
A6        = "Square root is:
B6        = IF(ITER=1,1,B8)
B8 H      = (B6+B3/B6)/2
B10       = ITER
```

Figure 11.2

```
      :       A       ::    B    :
 1
 2
 3    Square root of:      99.99
 4
 5
 6    Square root is: 9.999500
 7
 8
 9
10                            21
```

Figure 11.3

the /GI command again, but choosing the Delta option allows you to specify the number of iterations you wish to count, in the range of 1 to 99.

A generalized graph-plotting routine is described in the manual of Release 2.1 and it is worth while looking at this in detail here.

A graph in which one variable is a function of another is drawn using the X–Y graph type where the independent variable, referred to as **X** in SuperCalc3, is scaled horizontally and the dependent variable, referred to as **Y**, is scaled vertically.

Before any calculation takes place, the /GM command should be issued. This is the command to switch off automatic recalculation as soon as an entry is written into the spreadsheet. When this has been done recalculation will only take place when the ! character is keyed in, and this will be after all the information has been entered onto the sheet.

The number of steps to be performed by the iteration are defined in cell A6. In this case there are going to be 21 values of Y calculated at regularly increasing values of X. The step size is defined by calculating the range between the highest and lowest values of X, contained in cells A3 and A2, and then dividing this number by 20. (21 steps means 20 intervals.) The number of iterations is counted and displayed in cell E5 which contains the formula

```
IF(TRUE,ITER,E5)
```

since ITER is held outside the spreadsheet. By this means E5 is defined as a **circular cell** — note the reference CIRC in the top left-hand corner of the sheet. The contents of cell A5 will cause the calculation to stop as soon as the contents of cell E5, the iteration counter, exceed the contents of A6, the number of iterations to be performed. This is because this cell is designated as the cell containing Delta from the /GISD (Global, Iteration Control, Solve, Delta) option.

The next thing is to force the recalculation of X each time a new step is taken. This formula is placed in cell A9. It states that initially, when ITER is 1, X takes the value of A2, the lowest value. From then on X is incremented by the number stored in cell A7.

The function being graphed is entered in cell A14 and takes its variable from cell A9, which is the current value of X.

The contents of these cells are shown in Fig. 11.4a. Figure 11.4b shows the 'business end' of the calculation where column I contains the step numbers—only the first nineteen are displayed on the screen—the column actually extends down to row 22. Column J contains the values of X which start at the number stored in cell A2 and proceed incrementally by the contents of A7. Column K contains the calculated values of Y, the dependent variable. It tests the value of the iteration counter held in E5 against the entry in column I. If they are equal, then the number stored in cell

```
CIRC!    A    ||    B    ||    C    ||    D    ||    E    ||    F    ||    G   |
1
2      -2
3      2
4
5      IF(E5>=A6,1E62,0)                          IF(TRUE,ITER,E5)
6      21
7      (A3-A2)/(A6-1)
8
9      IF((ITER=1,A2,A9+A7)
10
11
12
13
14     COS(2*A9)
15
16
17
18
19
20
<A1
Width:   9   Memory:   74    Last Col/Row:K22          ? for HELP
  1>
F1=Help  F2=Cancel F9=Plot F10=View
```

Figure 11.4a

```
CIRC!    G    !!    H    !!    I    !!    J    !!    K    !!    L    !!    M    !
1
2                              1          A2          IF(E5=I2,A14,K2)
3                              2          J2+A7       IF(E5=I3,A14,K3)
4                              3          J3+A7       IF(E5=I4,A14,K4)
5                              4          J4+A7       IF(E5=I5,A14,K5)
6                              5          J5+A7       IF(E5=I6,A14,K6)
7                              6          J6+A7       IF(E5=I7,A14,K7)
8                              7          J7+A7       IF(E5=I8,A14,K8)
9                              8          J8+A7       IF(E5=I9,A14,K9)
10                             9          J9+A7       IF(E5=I10,A14,K10)
11                             10         J10+A7      IF(E5=I11,A14,K11)
12                             11         J11+A7      IF(E5=I12,A14,K12)
13                             12         J12+A7      IF(E5=I13,A14,K13)
14                             13         J13+A7      IF(E5=I14,A14,K14)
15                             14         J14+A7      IF(E5=I15,A14,K15)
16                             15         J15+A7      IF(E5=I16,A14,K16)
17                             16         J16+A7      IF(E5=I17,A14,K17)
18                             17         J17+A7      IF(E5=I18,A14,K18)
19                             18         J18+A7      IF(E5=I19,A14,K19)
20                             19         J19+A7      IF(E5=I20,A14,K20)
>N1
Width:   9   Memory:   74    Last Col/Row:K22          ? for HELP
  1>
F1=Help  F2=Cancel F9=Plot F10=View
```

Figure 11.4b

A14, the calculated value of Y for the current value of X, is displayed. If they are not equal, then the contents of the cell are unchanged. The result of this is that column K contains the values of Y and column J contains the values of X. From the /VD (View command, Data option) you can define the independent, X, variable as the contents of column J and the Y variable as the contents of column K. From /VG (View

```
Current graph (#1) -> X-  Current Device -> EPSON MX100 Printer

HEADINGS:                     SCALING:
Main:     (empty)             Y-Axis: Auto
Sub:      (empty)             X-Axis: Min = (A2), Max = (A3), 4 divisions
X-Axis:   (empty)
Y-Axis:   (empty)

TIME-LABELS: (empty)

   Data           Pt-Labels      Var-Labels      FORMATS:
A: (J2:J22)       (empty)        (empty)         Axis:
B: (K2:K22)       (empty)        (empty)         Time:
C: (empty)        (empty)        (empty)         Var:
D: (empty)        (empty)        (empty)         Point:
E: (empty)        (empty)        (empty)         % :
F: (empty)        (empty)        (empty)
G: (empty)        (empty)        (empty)
H: (empty)        (empty)        (empty)
I: (empty)        (empty)        (empty)
J: (empty)        (empty)        (empty)

PIE EXPLOSION: None                    MODE: One Variable (A)
F1 or <?> for AnswerScreen
F1=Help F2=Cancel F9=Plot F10=View
```

Figure 11.4c

command, Graph-type option), define the graph as an X–Y graph. In order to obtain the scale along the bottom, take the Options choice from the /V command and state that the X-axis is to be divided into four steps. The graph definition is shown in Fig. 11.4c.

The RAN function

This is a new SuperCalc3 mathematical function which generates a pseudo-random number in the range 0 to 1. In order to use this to generate a number in, say, the range 0 to 100, the form is

```
RAN*100
```

You could use this to generate random dates, for example, by combining RAN with DATE. DATE, as you may have discovered already, is always in US format (MM,DD,YY). Even if you use the EDAT form, where you enter the date in the DD,MM,YY format, it is still displayed in the American way! A random date in 1986 could then be generated by

```
DATE(RAN*12,RAN*30,86)
```

always assuming that every month has thirty days in it! To generate a closer approximation to a truly random date would need rather more detailed programming.

The SIDEWAYS program

In addition to the SDI program for data conversion, which now allows you to convert Lotus 1–2–3 and VisiCalc worksheets to and from SuperCalc3 format, there is another utility called SIDEWAYS which makes it possible for you to print very wide spreadsheets on your printer by turning them through ninety degrees and printing the top border vertically down the page and the vertical border across the page. In order to do this the spreadsheet to be printed has first of all to be Output, /O, to a disk file. This automatically gives it a .PRN extension. It is this file which is printed sideways.

```
                    S I D E W A Y S version 2.02

Printer selected:    Epson MX/FX/R

Vertical form size (inches):   11.00
Horizontal form size (inches): 8.00

Double strike:                   OFF
Character font:                NORMAL        5 x 15 dot matrix

Character spacing (dots):          1          12.00 characters per inch
Line spacing (dots):               3           6.66 lines per inch

Left margin (inches):           0.00
Top margin (inches):            0.00
Bottom margin (inches):         0.00             53 lines per page

Starting page:                     1
Enter name of print file:
Directory:   A:\

F1 for HELP                                      F10 to exit
```

Figure 11.5a

gives it a .PRN extension. It is this file which is printed sideways.

Before using SIDEWAYS you must tell the utility the type of printer you are using by using the SIDEINS program. Then you invoke the printing program by calling for SIDEWAYS. The screen produced is shown in Fig. 11.5a.

If you have .PRN files to print on a disk drive other than A: then you need to position the cursor onto the Directory line and enter the appropriate drive identifier with its sub-directory if it has one. Then you can place the cursor at the 'Enter name of print file' line and type in the name of the file to be printed. If you want to view all the available files, press the → key to scroll through the directory. The other options on this screen can be changed in the same way. A wide spreadsheet printed using SIDEWAYS is shown in Fig. 11.6.

Item	Product code	Order Date	Quantity	Unit price	VAT @ 15%	Total price	Customer No.	Date dispatched	Part order
15mm bolts	1545	6/ 1/1986	250	.25	9.38	71.88	5678	5/29/1986	Y
25mm nuts	2535	6/ 1/1986	175	.19	4.99	38.24	3245	6/11/1986	N
10mm washers	1025	4/15/1986	150	.09	2.03	15.53	1231	4/25/1986	N
20mm bolts	2045	8/ 8/1986	230	.36	12.42	95.22	6789	8/18/1986	N
15mm washers	1525	10/22/1986	500	.15	11.25	86.25	9087	11/ 1/1986	N
No. 1 flanges	1055	12/ 6/1985	56	2.75	23.10	177.10	3423	12/16/1985	N
4.5 hp motor	4567	5/22/1986	2	67.80	20.34	155.94	3245	6/ 1/1986	Y
white undercoat	1889	9/26/1986	1	3.66	.55	4.21	5566	10/ 6/1986	Y
pink primer	2027	2/13/1986	2	4.88	1.46	11.22	7215	2/23/1986	N
15 ft ladder	1544	3/25/1986	3	24.70	11.12	85.22	4353	4/ 4/1986	N
30m rope	3078	4/28/1986	1	12.60	1.89	14.49	3241	5/ 8/1986	N
30mm washers	3025	10/20/1986	100	.44	6.60	50.60	5543	10/30/1986	Y
sugar soap	1212	6/20/1986	2	.50	.15	1.15	3341	6/30/1986	N
13amp fuses	1399	11/13/1986	24	.05	.18	1.38	4353	11/23/1986	N
60 watt bulbs	6023	6/15/1986	144	.67	14.47	110.95	5621	6/25/1986	Y
bulb holders	1104	10/29/1986	36	.98	5.29	40.57	8976	11/ 8/1986	Y
2 in brushes	2054	2/26/1986	12	.75	1.35	10.35	4456	3/ 8/1986	N
paint stripper	3546	5/19/1986	2	2.56	.77	5.89	2763	5/29/1986	N

Figure 11.6

Appendix

Appendix

In this appendix are a number of SuperCalc spreadsheets, mainly of a mathematical nature, that do not fit into the main part of this Companion. The first four are designed to appeal possibly to teachers who are interested in finding new and interesting ways of illustrating a number of mathematical techniques.

Example 1

This example deals with the solution of a pair of simultaneous linear equations of the form

$$a_1X + b_1Y = c_1$$
$$a_2X + b_2Y = c_2$$

by substituting in the two formulae

$$X = \frac{c_1b_2 - c_2b_1}{a_1b_2 - a_2b_1}$$

$$Y = \frac{c_2a_1 - c_1a_2}{a_1b_2 - a_2b_1}$$

The contents of the spreadsheet that performs this are displayed in Fig. A1. The coefficients of the two equations are entered in cells A3, A4, C3, C4, F3 and F4. The formula to perform the calculations is shown beneath these, and beside the equations in the general form are the equations in such a form as to allow the plotting of the graph of the two straight lines, thus enabling a visible check to be made on the

SOLUTION OF SIMULTANEOUS EQUATIONS

3 X	+4Y	=	2		X	Y	Y
2 X	-6Y	=	10		-10	(F3-A3*H4)/C3	(F4-A4*H4)/C4
					10	(F3-A3*H5)/C3	(F4-A4*H5)/C4
X	=	(F4*C3-F3*C4)/(A4*C3-A3*C4)					
Y	=	(F3*A4-F4*A3)/(A4*C3-A3*C4)					

Figure A1

SOLUTION OF SIMULTANEOUS EQUATIONS

3X	4Y	=	2	X	Y	Y
2X	-6Y	=	10	-10	8	-5
				10	-7	1.666667
X	=	2				
Y	=	-1				

Figure A2

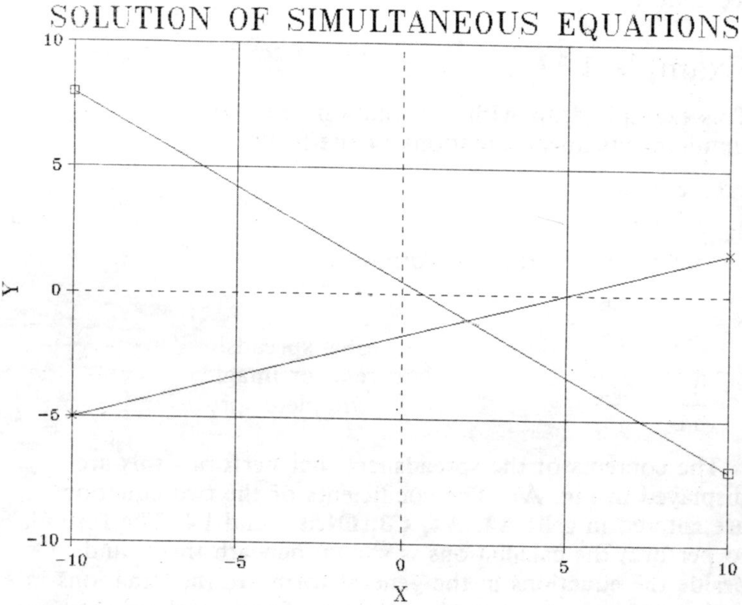

Figure A3

```
Current Graph (£1) -> X-Y  Current Device -> EPSON LQ1500 Printer

HEADINGS:                       SCALING:
Main:    (A1)                   Y-Axis: Auto
Sub:     (empty)                X-Axis: Auto
X-Axis: (H3)
Y-Axis: (I3)

TIME LABELS: (empty)

   Data            Pt-Labels        Var-Labels        FORMATS:
A: (H4:H5)        (empty)          (empty)           Axis:
B: (I4:I5)        (empty)          (empty)           Time:
C: (J4:J5)        (empty)          (empty)           Var:
D: (empty)        (empty)          (empty)           Point:
E: (empty)        (empty)          (empty)           % :
F: (empty)        (empty)          (empty)
G: (empty)        (empty)          (empty)
H: (empty)        (empty)          (empty)
I: (empty)        (empty)          (empty)
J: (empty)        (empty)          (empty)

PIE EXPLOSION: None               MODE: One Variable (A)
F1 or <?> for AnswerScreen.
F1=Help F2=Cancel F9=Plot F10=View
```

Figure A4

solutions. Figure A2 shows the display for the solution of the pair of equations

$$3X + 4Y = 2$$
$$2X - 6Y = 10$$

and their graphs are shown in Fig. A3. The specification of the graph is shown in Fig. A4.

Example 2

This example illustrates the use of a spreadsheet to solve a quadratic equation giving both real, or imaginary, roots when necessary. Figure A5 shows the complete spreadsheet with the solution of the general equation

$$aX^2 + bX + c = 0$$

making use of the traditional formula

$$X = \frac{-b \pm \sqrt{b^2 - 4ac}}{2a}$$

The coefficients are entered into cells A3, C3 and E3. The test for the discriminant, $b^2 - 4ac$, being positive or negative

```
SOLUTION OF QUADRATIC EQUATIONS
          A                    B                 C
 1        x^2        -5        x        1       =0

          REAL        IMAGINARY
      X1= IF((C3^2 IF((C3^2-4*A3*E3)<0,B9/(2*A3),0)
      X2= IF((C3^2 IF((C3^2-4*A3*E3)<0,-B9/(2*A3),0)

          IF((C3^2-4*A3*E3)>=0,SQRT(C3^2-4*A3*E3),SQRT(-(C3^2-4*A3*E3)))

   X          Y
 -10        A12^2*A3+A12*C3+E3
 A12+.5     A13^2*A3+A13*C3+E3
 A13+.5     A14^2*A3+A14*C3+E3
 A14+.5     A15^2*A3+A15*C3+E3
 A15+.5     A16^2*A3+A16*C3+E3
 A16+.5     A17^2*A3+A17*C3+E3
 A17+.5     A18^2*A3+A18*C3+E3
 A18+.5     A19^2*A3+A19*C3+E3
 A19+.5     A20^2*A3+A20*C3+E3
 A20+.5     A21^2*A3+A21*C3+E3
 A21+.5     A22^2*A3+A22*C3+E3
 A22+.5     A23^2*A3+A23*C3+E3
 A23+.5     A24^2*A3+A24*C3+E3
 A24+.5     A25^2*A3+A25*C3+E3
 A25+.5     A26^2*A3+A26*C3+E3
 A26+.5     A27^2*A3+A27*C3+E3
 A27+.5     A28^2*A3+A28*C3+E3
 A28+.5     A29^2*A3+A29*C3+E3
 A29+.5     A30^2*A3+A30*C3+E3
 A30+.5     A31^2*A3+A31*C3+E3
 A31+.5     A32^2*A3+A32*C3+E3
 A32+.5     A33^2*A3+A33*C3+E3
 A33+.5     A34^2*A3+A34*C3+E3
 A34+.5     A35^2*A3+A35*C3+E3
 A35+.5     A36^2*A3+A36*C3+E3
 A36+.5     A37^2*A3+A37*C3+E3
 A37+.5     A38^2*A3+A38*C3+E3
 A38+.5     A39^2*A3+A39*C3+E3
 A39+.5     A40^2*A3+A40*C3+E3
 A40+.5     A41^2*A3+A41*C3+E3
 A41+.5     A42^2*A3+A42*C3+E3
 A42+.5     A43^2*A3+A43*C3+E3
 A43+.5     A44^2*A3+A44*C3+E3
 A44+.5     A45^2*A3+A45*C3+E3
 A45+.5     A46^2*A3+A46*C3+E3
 A46+.5     A47^2*A3+A47*C3+E3
 A47+.5     A48^2*A3+A48*C3+E3
 A48+.5     A49^2*A3+A49*C3+E3
 A49+.5     A50^2*A3+A50*C3+E3
 A50+.5     A51^2*A3+A51*C3+E3
 A51+.5     A52^2*A3+A52*C3+E3
```

Figure A5

is carried out in cell E3 and the positive square root is then calculated in that cell using IF. The contents of this cell would, in practice, be hidden using the /F (Format command) and choosing the H option to hide the entry. The calculation of the real and imaginary parts takes place in cells B6 and B7. The calculations to create the data

SOLUTION OF QUADRATIC EQUATIONS

A	B	C
1x^2	-5x	1=0

	REAL	IMAGINARY
X1=	4.791288	0
X2=	.2087122	0

4.582576

X	Y
-10	151
-9.5	138.75
-9	127
-8.5	115.75
-8	105
-7.5	94.75
-7	85
-6.5	75.75
-6	67
-5.5	58.75
-5	51
-4.5	43.75
-4	37
-3.5	30.75
-3	25
-2.5	19.75
-2	15
-1.5	10.75
-1	7
-.5	3.75
0	1
.5	-1.25
1	-3
1.5	-4.25
2	-5
2.5	-5.25
3	-5
3.5	-4.25
4	-3
4.5	-1.25
5	1
5.5	3.75
6	7
6.5	10.75
7	15
7.5	19.75
8	25
8.5	30.75
9	37
9.5	43.75
10	51

Figure A6

for the graph that accompanies the solution is in the table beneath the main calculations.

The actual display solving the equation

$$X^2 - 5X + 1 = 0$$

is shown in Fig. A6.

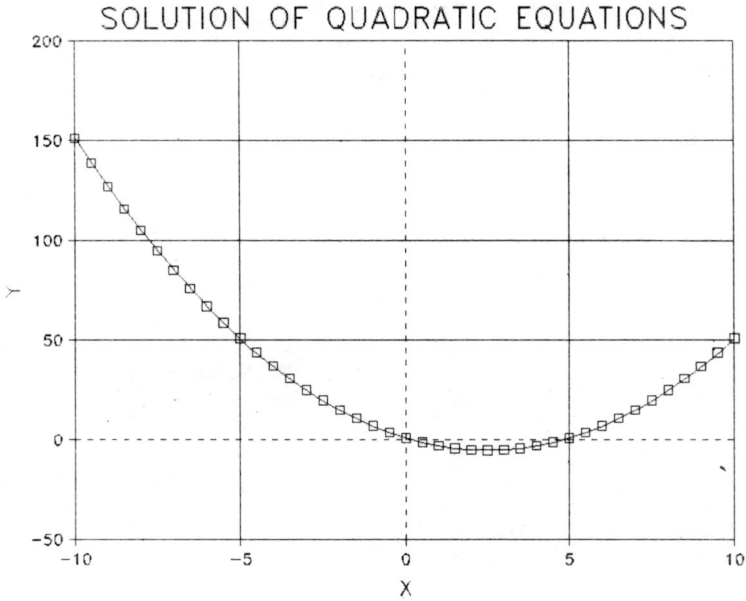

Figure A7

```
Current Graph (£1) -> X-Y  Current Device -> EPSON LQ1500 Printer

HEADINGS:                          SCALING:
Main:   (empty)                    Y-Axis: Auto
Sub:    (empty)                    X-Axis: Auto
X-Axis: (A11)
Y-Axis: (B11)

TIME LABELS: (empty)

   Data              Pt-Labels           Var-Labels           FORMATS:
A: (A12:A52)         (empty)             (empty)              Axis:
B: (B12:B52)         (empty)             (empty)              Time:
C: (empty)           (empty)             (empty)              Var:
D: (empty)           (empty)             (empty)              Point:
E: (empty)           (empty)             (empty)              % :
F: (empty)           (empty)             (empty)
G: (empty)           (empty)             (empty)
H: (empty)           (empty)             (empty)
I: (empty)           (empty)             (empty)
J: (empty)           (empty)             (empty)

PIE EXPLOSION: None                  MODE: One Variable (A)
F1 or <?> for AnswerScreen.
F1=Help F2=Cancel F9=Plot F10=View
```

Figure A8

The graph of the function is shown in Fig. A7 and the specification of the graph is shown in Fig. A8.

Example 3

There are of course many equations that cannot be solved by a straightforward formula. In this example, a cubic equation is chosen, although it would not be a difficult task to extend the method to solve equations of a higher degree. The method chosen in this case is that of successive approximations where the iterative facility of SuperCalc 3 Release 2 is made use of.

A first approximation to a solution is entered and this is successively refined until the iteration is allowed to cease.

The method is based on the fact that if you wish to solve the equation

$$aX^3 + bX^2 + cX + d = 0$$

then if a trial root is **k** then the value **k + h** is substituted in the original equation and the squared and cubed terms in **h** are ignored in order to gain a value for **h** from the linear equation that results. This value for **h** is added to **k** and a better approximation to the root is obtained.

The coefficients of the equation being solved are entered in cells A4, C4, E4 and G4 and the essential calculation is carried out in cell B9.

The recalculation switch was set to manual, /G (Global command) with the Manual option, so that the calculation has to be forced to commence. In addition, the iteration option was chosen from the same command and the number of iterations forced to stop at 20. This was to prevent pointless calculation when the root diverged.

The initial approximation is entered in cell D6 (in practice, this cell could be hidden from view as it has no real part in the answer) and the iteration test that starts the calculation off is in cell B7.

By pressing the ! (manual recalculation key) the iteration proceeds and the values in the table that produce the graph to illustrate the answer are produced.

```
SOLVING AN EQUATION
USING SUCCESSIVE APPROXIMATIONS

 1 X^3        0        X^2    3  X     -7 =0

First approximation = 1
X=   IF(ITER=1,D6,B9)
Next approximation
X=  B7-(G4+A4*B7^3+C4*B7^2+E4*B7)/(3*B7*A4+2*B7*C4+E4)
```

X	Y
-5	A4*I7^3+C4*I7^2+E4*I7+G4
I7+.25	A4*I8^3+C4*I8^2+E4*I8+G4
I8+.25	A4*I9^3+C4*I9^2+E4*I9+G4
I9+.25	A4*I10^3+C4*I10^2+E4*I10+G4
I10+.25	A4*I11^3+C4*I11^2+E4*I11+G4
I11+.25	A4*I12^3+C4*I12^2+E4*I12+G4
I12+.25	A4*I13^3+C4*I13^2+E4*I13+G4
I13+.25	A4*I14^3+C4*I14^2+E4*I14+G4
I14+.25	A4*I15^3+C4*I15^2+E4*I15+G4
I15+.25	A4*I16^3+C4*I16^2+E4*I16+G4
I16+.25	A4*I17^3+C4*I17^2+E4*I17+G4
I17+.25	A4*I18^3+C4*I18^2+E4*I18+G4
I18+.25	A4*I19^3+C4*I19^2+E4*I19+G4
I19+.25	A4*I20^3+C4*I20^2+E4*I20+G4
I20+.25	A4*I21^3+C4*I21^2+E4*I21+G4
I21+.25	A4*I22^3+C4*I22^2+E4*I22+G4
I22+.25	A4*I23^3+C4*I23^2+E4*I23+G4
I23+.25	A4*I24^3+C4*I24^2+E4*I24+G4
I24+.25	A4*I25^3+C4*I25^2+E4*I25+G4
I25+.25	A4*I26^3+C4*I26^2+E4*I26+G4
I26+.25	A4*I27^3+C4*I27^2+E4*I27+G4
I27+.25	A4*I28^3+C4*I28^2+E4*I28+G4
I28+.25	A4*I29^3+C4*I29^2+E4*I29+G4
I29+.25	A4*I30^3+C4*I30^2+E4*I30+G4
I30+.25	A4*I31^3+C4*I31^2+E4*I31+G4
I31+.25	A4*I32^3+C4*I32^2+E4*I32+G4
I32+.25	A4*I33^3+C4*I33^2+E4*I33+G4
I33+.25	A4*I34^3+C4*I34^2+E4*I34+G4
I34+.25	A4*I35^3+C4*I35^2+E4*I35+G4
I35+.25	A4*I36^3+C4*I36^2+E4*I36+G4
I36+.25	A4*I37^3+C4*I37^2+E4*I37+G4
I37+.25	A4*I38^3+C4*I38^2+E4*I38+G4
I38+.25	A4*I39^3+C4*I39^2+E4*I39+G4
I39+.25	A4*I40^3+C4*I40^2+E4*I40+G4
I40+.25	A4*I41^3+C4*I41^2+E4*I41+G4
I41+.25	A4*I42^3+C4*I42^2+E4*I42+G4
I42+.25	A4*I43^3+C4*I43^2+E4*I43+G4
I43+.25	A4*I44^3+C4*I44^2+E4*I44+G4
I44+.25	A4*I45^3+C4*I45^2+E4*I45+G4
I45+.25	A4*I46^3+C4*I46^2+E4*I46+G4
I46+.25	A4*I47^3+C4*I47^2+E4*I47+G4

Figure A9

Figure A9 shows the contents of the cells and Fig. A10 shows the display that produces the graph in Fig. A11.

In Fig. A12 is the graph specification.

```
SOLVING AN EQUATION
USING SUCCESSIVE APPROXIMATIONS

  1X^3                    0X^2      3X       -7=0

First approximation =     1                               X         Y
X=  1.406288                                              -5      -147
Next approximation                                     -4.75  -128.422
X=  1.406288                                            -4.5  -111.625
                                                       -4.25  -96.5156
                                                          -4       -83
                                                       -3.75  -70.9844
                                                        -3.5   -60.375
                                                       -3.25  -51.0781
                                                          -3       -43
                                                       -2.75  -36.0469
                                                        -2.5   -30.125
                                                       -2.25  -25.1406
                                                          -2       -21
                                                       -1.75  -17.6094
                                                        -1.5   -14.875
                                                       -1.25  -12.7031
                                                          -1       -11
                                                        -.75  -9.67188
                                                         -.5    -8.625
                                                        -.25  -7.76563
                                                           0        -7
                                                         .25  -6.23438
                                                          .5    -5.375
                                                         .75  -4.32813
                                                           1        -3
                                                        1.25  -1.29688
                                                         1.5      .875
                                                        1.75  3.609375
                                                           2         7
                                                        2.25  11.14063
                                                         2.5    16.125
                                                        2.75  22.04688
                                                           3        29
                                                        3.25  37.07813
                                                         3.5    46.375
                                                        3.75  56.98438
                                                           4        69
                                                        4.25  82.51563
                                                         4.5    97.625
                                                        4.75  114.4219
                                                           5       133
```

Figure A10

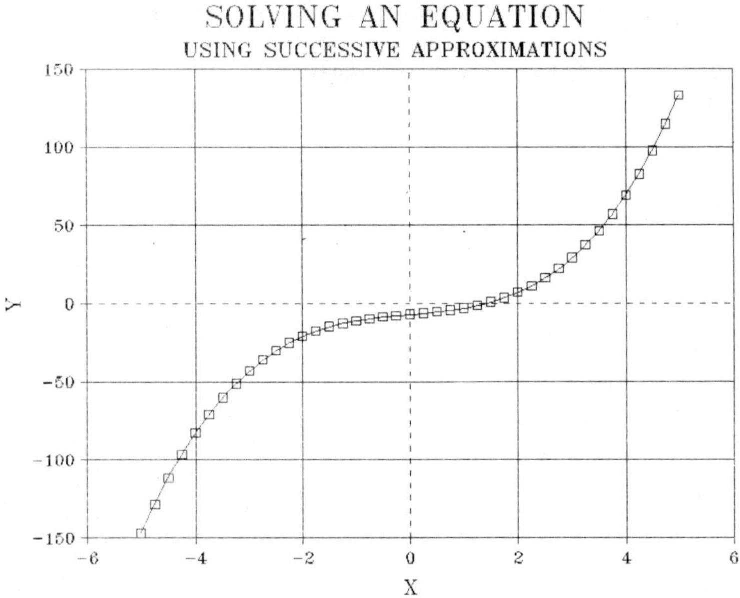

Figure A11

```
Current Graph (£1) -> X-Y  Current Device -> EPSON LQ1500 Printer

HEADINGS:                  SCALING:
Main:    (A1)              Y-Axis: Auto
Sub:     (A2)              X-Axis: Auto
X-Axis: (I6)
Y-Axis: (J6)

TIME LABELS: (empty)

   Data             Pt-Labels         Var-Labels        FORMATS:
A: (I7:I47)         (empty)           (empty)           Axis:
B: (J7:J47)         (empty)           (empty)           Time:
C: (empty)          (empty)           (empty)           Var:
D: (empty)          (empty)           (empty)           Point:
E: (empty)          (empty)           (empty)           % :
F: (empty)          (empty)           (empty)
G: (empty)          (empty)           (empty)
H: (empty)          (empty)           (empty)
I: (empty)          (empty)           (empty)
J: (empty)          (empty)           (empty)

PIE EXPLOSION: None               MODE: One Variable (A)
F1 or <?> for AnswerScreen.
F1=Help F2=Cancel F9=Plot F10=View
```

Figure A12

Example 4

The method used in the previous example does not always guarantee to find all the solutions of the equation. The method used in this example goes a long way towards finding more than one solution, as will be shown. It uses the method, ascribed to Newton, that uses the first derivative of the function to improve on an approximate root. If f(x) is the function and f'(x) is its derivative, then a better approximation, x_2, to the original approximation, x_1, is found from

$$x_2 = x_1 - \frac{f(x_1)}{f'(x_1)}$$

Again the coefficients are entered in cells A4, C4, E4 and G4 and the resulting formula to calculate the root is in cell B10. The iteration test is in cell B8 and the initial approximation is in cell E6. The contents of the cells are shown in Fig. A13, with three roots calculated in turn for the equation

$$X^3 + X^2 - 8X - 1 = 0$$

shown in Fig. A14

The iteration is set up in the same way as in Example 3.

```
SOLVING AN EQUATION
USING NEWTON'S METHOD

 1 X^3         0          X^2    -8 X      -1 =0

First approximation =       2

X = IF(ITER=1,E6,B10)

X = (2*A4*B8^3+C4*B8^2-G4)/(3*A4*B8^2+2*C4*B8+E4)
```

Figure A13

```
SOLVING AN EQUATION
USING NEWTON'S METHOD

  1X^3                    0X^2      -8X       -1=0

First approximation =               -2

X = -2.76372

X = -2.76372
```

```
SOLVING AN EQUATION
USING NEWTON'S METHOD

  1X^3                    0X^2      -8X       -1=0

First approximation =                0

X = -.125246

X = -.125246
```

```
SOLVING AN EQUATION
USING NEWTON'S METHOD

  1X^3                    0X^2      -8X       -1=0

First approximation =                2

X = 2.888969

X = 2.888969
```

Figure A14

Example 5

Numerical integration is a technique well suited to adaptation to a spreadsheet. In this example, the well-known Simpson's Rule is implemented. Trying to program such a process in a language such as BASIC can be very frustrating; SuperCalc takes all the effort out of it all.

The essential information is entered in four cells. These are C1 for the number of strips used, C3 and C4 for the lower and upper bounds of the integral and the definition of the function is held in cell D8. The expression in D8 makes reference to the contents of cell B6 in which is held the current value of variable X.

```
No. of strips =     16        IF((C1/2)=INT(C1/2),"OK","Not OK")

Lower bound =       -2                                 IF(F4=F5,1E62,0)
Upper bound =       2        Step size (C4-C3)/C1      ITER     (No. of iterations)
                                                       C1+1     (No. of steps)
X =        IF(ITER=1,C3,C3+(ITER-1)*(C4-C3)/C1)

Current value of function = EXP(-(B6^2)/2)

First ordinate =    IF(ITER=1,D8,C10+0)
Sum of all but first =       IF(ITER=1,0,D11+D8)
Sum of even ordinates =      IF(ITER=1,0,IF(ITER/2=INT(ITER/2),D12+D8,D12))

Area under curve = (C4-C3)/(3*C1)*(C10+2*D11+2*D12-D8)
```

Figure A15

```
No. of strips =             16        OK

Lower bound =               -2                      1e62
Upper bound =                2Step size   .25         17(No. of iterations)
                                                      17(No. of steps)
X =                 2

Current value of function = .1353353

First ordinate =    .1353353
Sum of all but first =      9.559038
Sum of even ordinates =     4.796343

Area under curve = 2.392563
```

Figure A16

The expression in D8 sets X to be the lower bound if the value of ITER, the iteration count, is one. Otherwise its value steps through the range increasing by the step size, (C4–C3)/C1, until the upper bound is reached. The termination of the iteration is effected by the entry in cell F3 that puts a flag, the number 1E62, in the cell when the number of iterations reaches the number of steps made in the calculation. This flag is implemented by choosing the Iteration option from the /G (Global command) and then the S followed by the D (Delta) option. At this point the value of Delta, the measure of convergence, is given as cell F3. At the same time the Manual recalculation can be chosen.

The value of the first ordinate is set in cell C10 and beneath it are the values of the sum of all but the first ordinates and the sum of the even ordinates. Note how the circular references are made to the cells themselves in order to increment their values by the appropriate amount each time. The rather non-standard way of expressing the Simpson Rule is used in order to simplify the calculation which is shown in cell C14.

The Rule is now expressed as

Step size divided by two multiplied by three times the first ordinate plus twice the sum of all but the first ordinate plus twice the sum of the even ordinates minus the last ordinate.

Lastly, the entry in cell D1 is merely to check that an even number of strips have been chosen, in which case the **OK** flag is displayed. Otherwise the **Not OK** flag shows.

The contents of the cells are shown in Fig. A15. Figure A16 shows the display after the evaluation of the integral of the function

e^{-x^2/2}

between the limits of −2 and 2 for 16 strips.

There are a number of cells whose entries could be hidden in this example, but they are all displayed in the interests of clarity.

Index

NOTES

NOTES

NOTES

NOTES

NOTES

NOTES

NOTES